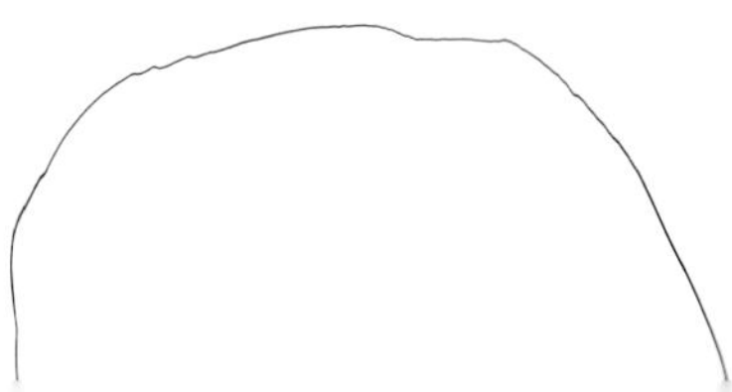

BUSINESS ECONOMICS IN A RAPIDLY-CHANGING WORLD

THE SMALL BUSINESS LENDING FUND

BUSINESS ECONOMICS IN A RAPIDLY-CHANGING WORLD

Additional books in this series can be found on Nova's website under the Series tab.

Additional E-books in this series can be found on Nova's website under the E-book tab.

BUSINESS ISSUES, COMPETITION AND ENTREPRENEURSHIP

Additional books in this series can be found on Nova's website under the Series tab.

Additional E-books in this series can be found on Nova's website under the E-book tab.

BUSINESS ECONOMICS IN A RAPIDLY-CHANGING WORLD

THE SMALL BUSINESS LENDING FUND

JOSHUA A. BELL
AND
CARL M. RICHARDSON
EDITORS

Nova Science Publishers, Inc.
New York

For permission to use material from this book please contact us:
Telephone 631-231-7269; Fax 631-231-8175
Web Site: http://www.novapublishers.com

Library of Congress Cataloging-in-Publication Data

ISBN: 978-1-62257-212-0

Published by Nova Science Publishers, Inc. † New York

CONTENTS

PREFACE

This book examines the Small Business Lending Fund, with a focus on the supply and demand for small business loans. Congressional interest in small businesses reflects, in part, concerns about economic growth and unemployment. Small businesses, defined as having fewer than 500 employees, have played an important role in net employment growth during previous economic recoveries. However, recent data show that net employment growth at small businesses is not increasing at the same rate as in previous economic recoveries. Some have argued that current economic conditions make it imperative that the federal government provide additional resources to assist small businesses in acquiring capital necessary to start, continue, or expand operations and create jobs. Others worry about the long-term adverse economic effects of spending programs that increase the federal deficit.

Chapter 1 - Congressional interest in small business access to capital reflects, in part, concerns about economic growth and unemployment. Small businesses, defined as having fewer than 500 employees, have played an important role in net employment growth during previous economic recoveries.

However, recent data show that net employment growth at small businesses is not increasing at the same rate as in previous economic recoveries.

Some, including President Obama, have argued that current economic conditions make it imperative that the federal government provide additional resources to assist small businesses in acquiring capital necessary to start, continue, or expand operations and create jobs. Others worry about the long-term adverse economic effects of spending programs that increase the federal deficit.

They advocate business tax reduction, reform of financial credit market regulation, and federal fiscal restraint as the best means to assist small businesses and create jobs.

Several laws were enacted during the 111th Congress to enhance small business access to capital. For example, P.L. 111-5, the American Recovery and Reinvestment Act of 2009 (ARRA), provided the Small Business Administration (SBA) an additional $730 million, including funding to temporarily subsidize SBA fees and increase the 7(a) loan guaranty program's maximum loan guaranty percentage to 90%. P.L. 111-240, the Small Business Jobs Act of 2010, authorized the Secretary of the Treasury to establish a $30 billion Small Business Lending Fund (SBLF) ($4.0 billion was issued) to encourage community banks with less than $10 billion in assets to increase their lending to small businesses, a $1.5 billion State Small Business Credit Initiative to provide funding to participating states with small business capital access programs, numerous changes to the SBA's loan guaranty and contracting programs, funding to continue the SBA's fee subsidies and the 7(a) program's 90% maximum loan guaranty percentage through December 31, 2010, and about $12 billion in tax relief for small businesses. P.L. 111-322, the Continuing Appropriations and Surface Transportation Extensions Act, 2011, authorized the SBA to continue its fee subsidies and the 7(a) program's 90% maximum loan guaranty percentage through March 4, 2011, or until available funding was exhausted, which occurred on January 3, 2011.

This report focuses on the SBLF. It opens with a discussion of the supply and demand for small business loans. The SBLF's advocates argued that the SBLF was needed to enhance the supply of small business loans.

The report then examines other arguments which were presented both for and against the program. Advocates argued that the SBLF would increase lending to small businesses and, in turn, create jobs.

Opponents argued that the SBLF could lose money, lacked sufficient oversight provisions, did not require lenders to increase their lending to small businesses, could serve as a vehicle for TARP recipients to effectively refinance their TARP loans on more favorable terms with little or any resulting benefit for small businesses, and could encourage a failing lender to make even riskier loans to avoid higher dividend payments.

The report concludes with an examination of the program's implementation and a discussion of bills introduced during the 112th Congress to amend the SBLF. For example, S. 681, the Greater Accountability in the

Lending Fund Act of 2011, would limit the program's authority to 15 years from enactment and prohibit TARP recipients from participating in the program. H.R. 2807, the Small Business Leg-Up Act of 2011, would transfer any unobligated and repaid funds from the SBLF to the Community Development Financial Institutions Fund "to increase the availability of credit for small businesses." H.R. 3147, the Small Business Lending Extension Act, would extend the Treasury Department's investment authority from one year to two years.

Chapter 2 - Small businesses are a vital part of the American economy and their success is a critical component of the economic recovery. Established by the Small Business Jobs Act of 2010 (the Act), the Small Business Lending Fund (SBLF) is a dedicated fund designed to provide capital to qualified community banks and community development loan funds (CDLFs) in order to encourage small business lending. The purpose of the SBLF is to encourage Main Street banks and small businesses to work together, help create jobs, and promote economic growth in communities across the nation.

This report provides information on changes in small business lending by SBLF participants as of December 31, 2011, relative to baseline levels. Additionally, this report provides information on changes in business lending and other lending by SBLF banks, including a comparison of increases in business lending by these banks, a group of non-SBLF banks, and the subset of SBLF banks that refinanced into the program from Treasury's Capital Purchase Program (CPP).

As of December 31, 2011, institutions participating in SBLF have made important progress in increasing their small business lending, helping to support small businesses and local economies across the nation.

Chapter 3 - The Small Business Jobs Act of 2010 aimed to stimulate job growth by establishing the Small Business Lending Fund program (SBLF) within the U.S. Department of the Treasury (Treasury), among other activities. The SBLF program was designed to encourage community banks and community development loan funds with assets of less than $10 billion to increase their lending to small businesses.

The act also requires GAO to audit SBLF annually. This initial report examines (1) Treasury's procedures for evaluating applications for SBLF funds, (2) characteristics of institutions that applied for and received funds from SBLF and factors that influenced banks' decision to participate, and (3) Treasury's plans to monitor participants and measure SBLF's progress in increasing small business lending. GAO reviewed documents on Treasury's procedures and controls; analyzed data on applicants; compared SBLF banks with a peer group of nonparticipating banks; surveyed a representative sample of banks (for a weighted response rate of 66 percent); and interviewed Treasury, federal banking regulators, and representatives from industry associations.

Chapter 4 - This report presents the results of our audit of the investment decision process for the Small Business Lending Fund (SBLF) and provides an overview of the program's status. SBLF is a $30 billion fund that was created to provide capital to community banks with assets of less than $10 billion with incentives to stimulate small business lending. Our audit objectives were to determine whether: (1) the decision process established by Treasury ensures that eligible institutions in need of capital or with the most potential for small business lending are approved, and (2) investments are made in institutions with good track records for performance and compliance with small business lending requirements.

In: The Small Business Lending Fund ISBN 978-1-62257-212-0
Editors: J. A. Bell and C. M. Richardson

Chapter 1

THE SMALL BUSINESS LENDING FUND*

Robert Jay Dilger

SUMMARY

Congressional interest in small business access to capital reflects, in part, concerns about economic growth and unemployment. Small businesses, defined as having fewer than 500 employees, have played an important role in net employment growth during previous economic recoveries.

However, recent data show that net employment growth at small businesses is not increasing at the same rate as in previous economic recoveries.

Some, including President Obama, have argued that current economic conditions make it imperative that the federal government provide additional resources to assist small businesses in acquiring capital necessary to start, continue, or expand operations and create jobs. Others worry about the long-term adverse economic effects of spending programs that increase the federal deficit.

They advocate business tax reduction, reform of financial credit market regulation, and federal fiscal restraint as the best means to assist small businesses and create jobs.

Several laws were enacted during the 111th Congress to enhance small business access to capital. For example, P.L. 111-5, the American

* This is an edited, reformatted and augmented version of a Congressional Research Service publication, CRS Report for Congress R42045, from www.crs.gov, prepared for Members and Committees of Congress, dated January 27, 2012.

Recovery and Reinvestment Act of 2009 (ARRA), provided the Small Business Administration (SBA) an additional $730 million, including funding to temporarily subsidize SBA fees and increase the 7(a) loan guaranty program's maximum loan guaranty percentage to 90%. P.L. 111-240, the Small Business Jobs Act of 2010, authorized the Secretary of the Treasury to establish a $30 billion Small Business Lending Fund (SBLF) ($4.0 billion was issued) to encourage community banks with less than $10 billion in assets to increase their lending to small businesses, a $1.5 billion State Small Business Credit Initiative to provide funding to participating states with small business capital access programs, numerous changes to the SBA's loan guaranty and contracting programs, funding to continue the SBA's fee subsidies and the 7(a) program's 90% maximum loan guaranty percentage through December 31, 2010, and about $12 billion in tax relief for small businesses. P.L. 111-322, the Continuing Appropriations and Surface Transportation Extensions Act, 2011, authorized the SBA to continue its fee subsidies and the 7(a) program's 90% maximum loan guaranty percentage through March 4, 2011, or until available funding was exhausted, which occurred on January 3, 2011.

This report focuses on the SBLF. It opens with a discussion of the supply and demand for small business loans. The SBLF's advocates argued that the SBLF was needed to enhance the supply of small business loans.

The report then examines other arguments which were presented both for and against the program. Advocates argued that the SBLF would increase lending to small businesses and, in turn, create jobs.

Opponents argued that the SBLF could lose money, lacked sufficient oversight provisions, did not require lenders to increase their lending to small businesses, could serve as a vehicle for TARP recipients to effectively refinance their TARP loans on more favorable terms with little or any resulting benefit for small businesses, and could encourage a failing lender to make even riskier loans to avoid higher dividend payments.

The report concludes with an examination of the program's implementation and a discussion of bills introduced during the 112th Congress to amend the SBLF. For example, S. 681, the Greater Accountability in the Lending Fund Act of 2011, would limit the program's authority to 15 years from enactment and prohibit TARP recipients from participating in the program. H.R. 2807, the Small Business Leg-Up Act of 2011, would transfer any unobligated and repaid funds from the SBLF to the Community Development Financial Institutions Fund "to increase the availability of credit for small businesses." H.R. 3147, the Small Business Lending Extension Act, would extend the Treasury Department's investment authority from one year to two years.

SMALL BUSINESS AND JOB CREATION

Congressional interest in small business access to capital reflects, in part, concerns about economic growth and unemployment.[1] Small businesses, defined as having fewer than 500 employees, have played an important role in net job growth during previous economic recoveries, particularly in the construction, housing, and retail sectors.[2] For example, after the eight-month recession that began in July 1990 and ended in March 1991, small businesses increased their net employment in the first year after the recession, while larger businesses continued to experience declines in employment.[3] In the recession that began in March 2001 and ended in November 2001, small businesses added 1.15 million net new jobs while larger businesses lost 0.15 million net new jobs.[4] Small businesses accounted for almost 60% of the net job losses during the December 2007-June 2009 recession.[5] Following the recession, small businesses continued to lose jobs for three consecutive quarters (-1.0 million jobs), as did larger firms (-522,000 jobs).[6] Since then, small businesses have been adding jobs (1.0 million jobs from June 30th of 2010 through September 30th of 2011) more rapidly than larger businesses (563,000 jobs from June 30th of 2010 through September 30th of 2011), but more slowly than in previous recoveries.[7]

The Federal Deposit Insurance Corporation has maintained comparable small business lending data for the second quarter (June 30th) of each year since 2002. *Figure 1* shows the amount of outstanding small business loans as of June 30th for each year since 2005. As shown in *Figure 1*, the amount of outstanding small business loans peaked at $711.5 billion as of June 30, 2008, and had decreased by 14.7% (-$104.5 billion) to $607.0 billion as of June 30, 2011.[8] Since then, the amount of outstanding small business loans has continued to fall, to $599.7 billion as of September 30, 2011.[9] As a result, there has been increased concern in Congress that small businesses might be prevented from accessing sufficient capital to enable them to lead job growth during the current recovery.

Some, including President Obama, have argued that current economic conditions make it imperative that the federal government provide additional resources to assist small businesses in acquiring capital necessary to start, continue, or expand operations and create jobs. Others worry about the long-term adverse economic effects of spending programs that increase the federal deficit. They advocate business tax reduction, reform of financial credit market regulation, and federal fiscal restraint as the best means to assist small businesses and create jobs.

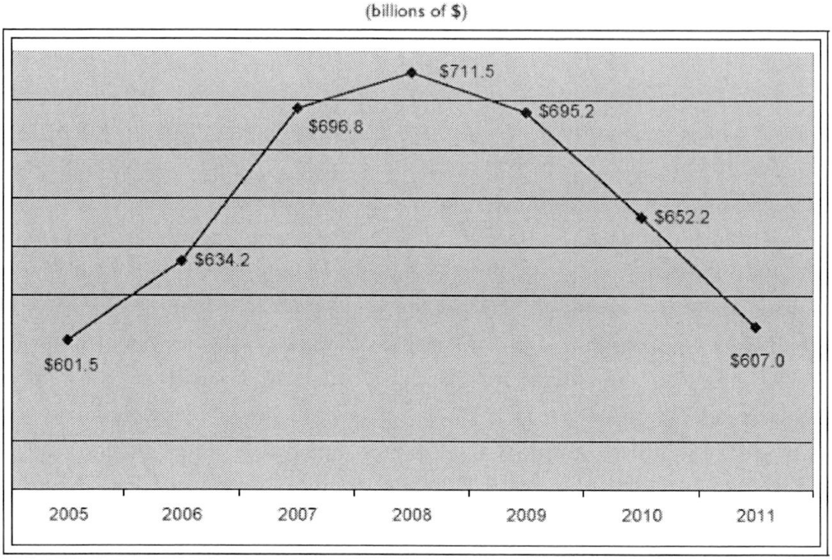

Source: Federal Deposit Insurance Corporation, "Statistics on Depository Institutions," Washington, DC, http://www2.fdic.gov/SDI/main.asp.

Note: Data as of June 30 each year.

Figure 1. Outstanding Small Business Loans, 2005-2011.

Several laws were enacted during the 111th Congress to enhance small business access to capital. For example, P.L. 111-5, the American Recovery and Reinvestment Act of 2009 (ARRA), provided the Small Business Administration (SBA) an additional $730 million, including $375 million to temporarily subsidize SBA fees and increase the 7(a) loan guaranty program's maximum loan guaranty percentage from 85% on loans of $150,000 or less and 75% on loans exceeding $150,000 to 90% for all regular 7(a) loans. P.L. 111-240, the Small Business Jobs Act of 2010, authorized the Secretary of the Treasury to establish a $30 billion Small Business Lending Fund (SBLF) ($4.0 billion was issued) to encourage community banks with less than $10 billion in assets to increase their lending to small businesses, a $1.5 billion State Small Business Credit Initiative to provide funding to participating states with small business capital access programs, numerous changes to the SBA's loan guaranty and contracting programs, funding to continue the SBA's fee subsidies and the 7(a) program's 90% maximum loan guaranty percentage through December 31, 2010, and about $12 billion in tax relief for small businesses. P.L. 111-322, the Continuing Appropriations and Surface Transportation Extensions Act, 2011, authorized the SBA to continue its fee subsidies and the 7(a) program's 90% maximum loan guaranty percentage through March 4, 2011, or until available funding was exhausted, which occurred on January 3, 2011.

According to the SBA, the temporary fee subsidies and 90% maximum loan guaranty for the 7(a) program "engineered a significant turnaround in SBA lending.... The end result is that the agency helped put more than $42 billion in the hands of small businesses through the Recovery Act and Jobs Act combined."[10]

This report focuses on the SBLF. It begins with a discussion of the supply and demand for small business loans. The SBLF's advocates argued that the SBLF was an important part of a larger effort to enhance the supply of small business loans. After describing the program's structure, the report then examines other arguments that were presented both for and against the program's enactment.

Advocates argued that the SBLF would increase lending to small businesses and, in turn, create jobs.

Opponents argued that the SBLF could lose money, lacked sufficient oversight provisions, did not require lenders to increase their lending to small businesses, could serve as a vehicle for TARP recipients to effectively refinance their TARP loans on more favorable terms with little or any resulting benefit for small businesses, and could encourage a failing lender to make even riskier loans to avoid higher dividend payments.

The report concludes with an examination of the SBLF's implementation by the Department of the Treasury and a discussion of bills introduced during the 112th Congress to amend the SBLF.

For example, S. 681, the Greater Accountability in the Lending Fund Act of 2011, would, among other provisions, limit the program's authority to 15 years from enactment and prohibit TARP recipients from participating in the program.

H.R. 2807, the Small Business Leg-Up Act of 2011, would transfer any unobligated and repaid funds from the SBLF when its investment authority expires on September 27, 2011, to the Community Development Financial Institutions Fund "to continue the program of making capital investments in eligible community development financial institutions in order to increase the availability of credit for small businesses."[11] H.R. 3147, the Small Business Lending Extension Act, would, among other provisions, extend the Treasury Department's investment authority from one year following the date of enactment to two years.

The Supply and Demand for Small Business Loans

Each quarter, the Federal Reserve Board surveys senior loan officers concerning their bank's lending practices. The survey includes questions about both the supply and demand for small business loans. For example, the survey includes a question concerning their bank's credit standards for small business loans: "Over the past three months, how have your bank's credit standards for approving applications for C&I [commercial and industrial] loans or credit lines— other than those to be used to finance mergers and acquisitions—for small firms (defined as having annual sales of less than $50 million) changed?" The senior loan officers are asked to indicate if their bank's credit standards have "Tightened considerably," "Tightened somewhat," "Remained basically unchanged," "Eased somewhat," or "Eased considerably." Subtracting the percentage of respondents reporting "Eased somewhat" and "Eased considerably" from the percentage of respondents reporting "Tightened considerably" and "Tightened somewhat" provides an indication of the market's supply of small business loans.

As shown on *Figure 2,* senior loan officers reported that they tightened small business credit standards from 2000-2004, loosened them from 2004-late 2006, tightened them somewhat in 2007, and tightened them considerably in 2008 and 2009.[12] Since 2009, senior loan officers report that they have eased their small business credit standards somewhat, and most senior loan officers report that they are no longer tightening those standards. However, the Federal Reserve Board notes that those lending standards "remain quite stringent following the prolonged and widespread tightening that took place over the past few years."[13]

The survey also includes a question concerning the demand for small business loans: "Apart from normal seasonal variation, how has demand for C&I loans changed over the past three months for small firms (annual sales of less than $50 million)?" Senior loan officers are asked to indicate if demand was "Substantially stronger," "Moderately stronger," "About the same," "Moderately weaker," or "Substantially weaker." Subtracting the percentage of respondents reporting "Moderately weaker" and "Substantially weaker" from the percentage of respondents reporting "Substantially stronger" and "Moderately stronger" provides an indication of the market's demand for small business loans.

As shown on *Figure 2*, senior loan officers reported that the demand for small business loans declined from 2000-2004, increased from 2004-late 2006, declined somewhat in 2007 and 2008, and declined significantly in 2009.

Demand then leveled off (at a relatively reduced level) during the first half of 2010, declined somewhat during the third quarter of 2010, increased somewhat during the fourth quarter of 2010 and into 2011, and then declined somewhat during the latter half of 2011.[14]

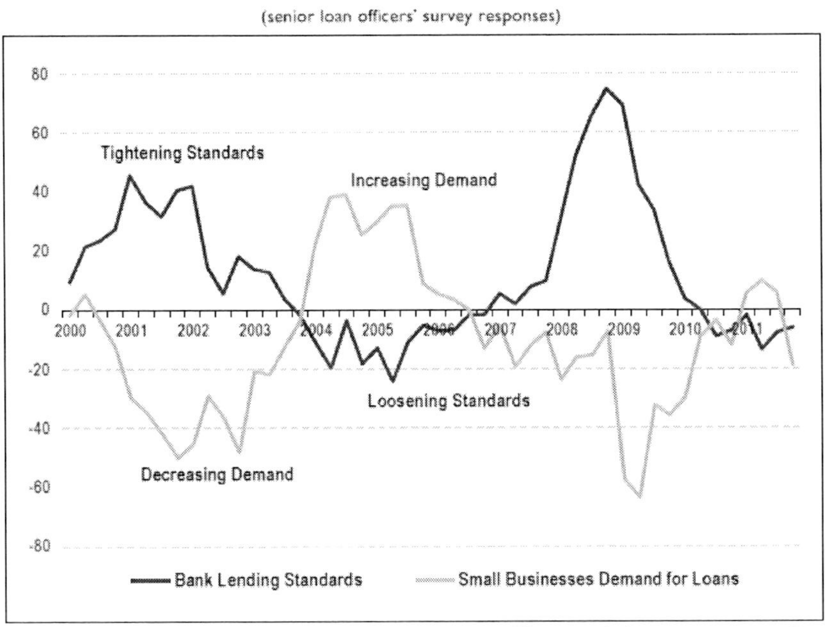

Source: Federal Reserve Board, "Senior Loan Officer Opinion Survey on Bank Lending Practices," Washington, DC, http://www.federalreserve.gov/boarddocs/SnLoanSurvey/; and Brian Headd, "Forum Seeks Solutions To Thaw Frozen Small Business Credit," The Small Business Advocate, vol. 28, no. 10 (December 2009), p. 3, http://www.sba.gov /sites/default/files/The%20Small%20Business%20Advocate%20-%20December%202009.pdf.

Figure 2. Small Business Lending Environment, 2000-2011.

Factors that May Have Contributed to the Decline in the Supply of Small Business Loans

According to an SBA-sponsored study of small business lending, several factors have contributed to the recent decline in small business lending.[15] The report's authors noted that the 30% decline in home prices from their peak in 2006 to 2010 diminished the value of collateral for many small business borrowers.

Many small business owners had relied on home equity loans to finance their small businesses during the real estate boom. They concluded that the absence of this additional source of collateral may have contributed to a decline in lending to small businesses.[16]

They also argued that many small businesses found it increasingly difficult to renew existing lines of credit as lenders became more cautious as a result of slow economic growth and an increasing risk of loan defaults, especially among small business startups which are generally considered among the most risky investments.[17] About half of all new small businesses fail in their first year.

They also argued that

- in this newly regulated market, smaller lenders are likely to be less profitable because they have fewer sales of products and services to spread out over the higher auditing and FDIC costs. Hence, they have less money to lend to small businesses and others, and
- the relative difficulty in assessing creditworthiness due to the lack of information about potential financial performance is very high in small business lending, especially in financial markets driven by factor—rather than relationship— lending. Therefore, one would expect the small business loan market to recover more slowly than other financial markets.[18]

The authors also noted that FDIC data indicated that in recent years small business lending had not only declined in absolute terms (the total amount of dollars borrowed and the total number of small business loans issued), but in relative terms as well (the market share of business loans):

> Over the eight years from 2003 through 2010, small business loans as a share of total business loans declined by more than 12 percentage points, from 81.7% in 2003 to 68.9% in 2010. Perhaps of most concern is the further decline in the ratios of small business loans to total assets and small business loans to total business loans. Small business loans constituted about 16.8% of total assets in 2005, but only 15.3% in 2010; hence, small business lending is becoming less significant for these lenders. Small business lending is also losing market share in the business loan market. In the eight-year period from 2003 to 2010, small business loans as a share of total business loans declined more than 10 percentage points from 81.7% in 2003 to 68.9% in 2010.[19]

Factors that May Have Contributed to the Decline in the Demand for Small Business Loans

According to the previously mentioned SBA-sponsored study of small business lending, the demand for small business loans fell during the recession primarily because many small businesses experienced a decline in sales, and many small business owners had a heightened level of uncertainty concerning future sales. The study's authors argued that given small business owners' lack of confidence in the demand for their goods and services, many small business owners decided to save capital instead of hiring additional employees and borrowing capital to invest in business expansions and inventory.[20]

The responses of small business owners to a monthly survey by the National Federation of Independent Business Research Foundation (NFIB) concerning small business owner's views of the economy support the argument that declining sales contributed to the decline in the demand for small business loans. Since 2008, small business owners responding to the NFIB surveys have identified poor sales as their number one problem. Prior to 2008, taxes had been reported as their number one problem in nearly every survey since the monthly surveys began in 1986.[21] Also, employment data suggests that small businesses were particularly hard hit by the recession. As mentioned previously, small businesses accounted for almost 60% of the net job losses during the December 2007-June 2009 recession.[22]

According to testimony by the Secretary of the Treasury before the House Small Business Committee on June 22, 2011, small businesses were especially hard hit by the recession because

> Small businesses are concentrated in sectors that were especially hard hit by the recession and the bursting of the housing bubble: construction and real estate. More than one-third of all construction workers are employed by firms with less than 20 workers, and an additional third are employed by businesses with fewer than 100 employees. Just over half of those employed in the real estate, rental, and leasing sectors work for businesses with less than 100 workers on their payrolls. More broadly, the rate of job losses was almost twice as high in small businesses as it was in larger firms during the depths of the crisis.[23]

Also, as mentioned previously, in recent months small businesses have been adding jobs more rapidly than larger businesses. However, they are adding jobs more slowly than in previous economic recoveries.[24]

The Congressional Response to the Decline in the Supply and Demand for Small Business Loans

During the 111th Congress, legislation designed to increase both the supply and demand for small business loans was adopted. For example, Congress provided over $1.1 billion to temporarily subsidize fees for the SBA's 7(a) and 504/CDC loan guaranty programs and to increase the 7(a) program's maximum loan guaranty percentage from 85% on loans of $150,000 or less and 75% on loans exceeding $150,000 to 90% for all regular 7(a) loans (funding was exhausted on January 3, 2011).[25] The fee subsidies were designed to increase the demand for small business loans by reducing the cost of borrowing. The 90% loan guarantee was designed to increase the supply of small business loans by reducing the risk of lending.

Congress also provided the SBA additional resources to expand its lending to small businesses. For example, ARRA included a $255 million temporary, two-year small business stabilization program to guarantee loans of $35,000 or less to small businesses for qualified debt consolidation, later named the America's Recovery Capital (ARC) Loan program (the program ceased issuing new loan guarantees on September 30, 2010); an additional $15 million for the SBA's surety bond program and a temporary increase in that program's maximum bond amount from $2 million to $5 million, and up to $10 million under certain conditions (the higher maximum bond amounts ended on September 30, 2010); an additional $6 million for the SBA's Microloan program's lending program and an additional $24 million for the Microloan program's technical assistance program; and increased the funds ("leverage") available to SBA-licensed Small Business Investment Companies (SBICs) to no more than 300% of the company's private capital or $150,000,000, whichever is less.[26]

Several other programs were also enacted during the 111th Congress to increase the supply of small business loans. For example, ARRA authorized the SBA to establish a temporary secondary market guarantee authority to provide a federal guarantee for pools of first lien 504/CDC program loans that are to be sold to third-party investors. ARRA also authorized the SBA to make below market interest rate direct loans to SBA-designated "Systemically Important Secondary Market (SISM) Broker-Dealers" who would use the loan funds to purchase SBA-guaranteed loans from commercial lenders, assemble them into pools, and sell them to investors in the secondary loan market.[27]

P.L. 111-240, the Small Business Jobs Act of 2010, extended the SBA's secondary market guarantee authority from two years after the date of

ARRA's enactment to two years after the date of the program's first sale of a pool of first lien position 504/CDC loans to a third-party investor (which took place on September 24, 2010).[28] The act also increased the loan guarantee limits for the SBA's 7(a) program from $2 million to $5 million, and for the 504/CDC program from $1.5 million to $5 million for "regular" borrowers, from $2 million to $5 million if the loan proceeds are directed toward one or more specified public policy goals, and from $4 million to $5.5 million for manufacturers. It also increased the SBA's Microloan program's loan limit for borrowers from $35,000 to $50,000 and for microlender intermediaries after their first year in the program from $3.5 million to $5 million.29 It also temporarily increased for one year (through September 26, 2011) the SBA 7(a) Express Program's loan limit from $350,000 to $1 million. The act also authorized the Secretary of the Treasury to establish the $30 billion SBLF and a $1.5 billion State Small Business Credit Initiative to provide funding to participating states with small business capital access programs.

THE SBLF'S LEGISLATIVE ORIGIN

On March 16, 2009, President Obama announced the first SBLF-like proposal. Under that proposal, the Department of the Treasury would have used TARP funds to purchase up to $15 billion of SBA-guaranteed loans.[30] The purchases were intended to "immediately unfreeze the secondary market for SBA loans and increase the liquidity of community banks."[31] The plan was dropped after it met resistance from lenders. Some lenders objected to TARP's requirement that participating lenders comply with executive compensation limits and issue warrants to the federal government. Smaller, community banks objected to the program's paperwork requirements, such as the provision of a small-business lending plan and quarterly reports.[32]

In his January 2010 State of the Union address, President Obama proposed the creation of a $30 billion SBLF to enhance access to credit for small businesses:

> when you talk to small business owners in places like Allentown, Pennsylvania, or Elyria, Ohio, you find out that even though banks on Wall Street are lending again, they're mostly lending to bigger companies. Financing remains difficult for small business owners across the country, even those that are making a profit.

> Tonight, I'm proposing that we take $30 billion of the money Wall Street banks have repaid and use it to help community banks give small businesses the credit they need to stay afloat.[33]

In response to the opposition community lenders had expressed concerning TARP's restrictions in 2009, the Obama Administration proposed that Congress approve legislation authorizing the transfer of up to $30 billion in TARP spending authority to the SBLF, and statutorily establish the new program as distinct and independent from TARP and its restrictions.[34] The Administration's legislative proposal was finalized and sent to Congress on May 7, 2010.[35]

Representative Barney Frank, then-chair of the House Committee on Financial Services, introduced H.R. 5297, the Small Business Lending Fund Act of 2010, on May 13, 2010.

The House Committee on Financial Services held a hearing on H.R. 5297 on May 18, 2010, and passed it, as amended to include a State Small Business Credit Initiative, the following day. The House passed the bill, as amended to include a Small Business Early-Stage Investment Program, a Small Business Borrower Assistance Program, and some small business tax reduction provisions, on June 17, 2010.

THE HOUSE-PASSED VERSION OF THE SBLF

Title I of the House-passed version of H.R. 5297 authorized the Secretary of the Treasury to establish a $30 billion SBLF "to address the ongoing effects of the financial crisis on small businesses by providing temporary authority to the Secretary of the Treasury to make capital investments in eligible institutions" with total assets equal to or less than $1 billion or $10 billion (as of the end of the fourth quarter of calendar year 2009) "in order to increase the availability of credit for small businesses."[36]

The authority to make capital investments in eligible institutions was limited to one year after enactment.

Eligible financial institutions having total assets equal to or less than $1 billion as of the end of the fourth quarter of calendar year 2009 could apply to receive a capital investment from the SBLF in an amount not exceeding 5% of risk-weighted assets, as reported in the FDIC call report immediately preceding the date of application. During the fourth quarter of 2009, 7,340 FDIC-insured lending institutions reported having assets amounting to less than $1 billion.[37] Eligible financial institutions having total assets equal to or less than $10 billion as of the end of the fourth quarter of calendar year 2009 could apply to receive a capital investment from the fund in an amount not exceeding 3% of risk-weighted assets, as reported in the FDIC call report immediately preceding the date of application. During the fourth quarter of 2009, 565 FDIC-insured lending institutions reported having assets of $1 billion to $10 billion.[38]

Risk-weighted assets are assets such as cash, loans, investments, and other financial institution assets that have different risks associated with them. FDIC regulations (12 C.F.R. §567.6) establish that cash and government bonds have a 0% risk-weighting; residential mortgage loans have a 50% risk-weighting; other types of assets (such as small business loans) have a higher risk-weighting.[39]

Lending institutions on the FDIC problem bank list, or institutions that have been removed from the FDIC problem bank list for less than 90 days were ineligible to participate in the program. Lending institutions could refinance securities issued through the Treasury Capital Purchase Program (CPP) and the Community Development Capital Incentive (CDCI) program under TARP, but only if the institution had not missed more than one dividend payment due under those programs. Participating banks would be charged a dividend rate of 5% per annum initially, with reduced rates available if the bank increased its small business lending. For example, during any calendar quarter in the initial two years of the capital investments under the program, the bank's rate would be lowered if it had increased its small business lending compared to the average small business lending it made in the four previous quarters immediately preceding the enactment of the bill, minus some allowable adjustments. A 2.5% to 5% increase in small business lending would have lowered the rate to 4%, a 5% to 7.5% increase would have lowered the rate to 3%, a 7.5% to 10% increase would have lowered the rate to 2%, and an increase greater than 10% would have lowered the rate to 1%. *Table 1* shows the dividend rates associated with small business lending increases by financial institutions. SBLF applicants were also required to submit a small business lending plan to the appropriate federal banking agency and, for applicants that are state-chartered banks, to the appropriate state banking regulator.

The plan was to describe how the applicant's business strategy and operating goals will allow it to address the needs of small businesses in the areas it serves, as well as a plan to provide linguistically and culturally appropriate outreach, where appropriate.

Table 1. Small Business Lending Increases and Dividend Rates Under the House-Passed Version of H.R. 5297

Small Business Lending Increase	Dividend Rate
10% or greater	1%
at least 7.5% but less than 10%	2%
at least 5% but less than 7.5%	3%
at least 2.5% but less than 5%	4%
Less than 2.5%	5%
No increase	7%

Source: H.R. 5297, the Small Business Jobs and Credit Act of 2010, Sec. 103. Small Business Lending Fund.

Note: The dividend rate would increase to 9% at the end of the five-year period that begins on the date of the capital investment under the program. The Senate-passed version of H.R. 5297, which became the Small Business Jobs Act of 2010, authorizes the same dividend rates.

The plan was to be treated as confidential supervisory information. The Secretary of the Treasury was required to consult with the appropriate federal banking agency or, in the case of an eligible institution that is a non-depository community development financial institution, the Community Development Financial Institution Fund, before determining if the eligible institution was to participate in the program.[40]

The bill specified that the SBLF would be "established as separate and distinct from the Troubled Asset Relief Program established by the Emergency Economic Stabilization Act of 2008. An institution shall not, by virtue of a capital investment under the Small Business Lending Fund Program, be considered a recipient of the Troubled Asset Relief Program."[41]

The bill also directed that all funds received by the Secretary of the Treasury in connection with purchases made by the SBLF, "including interest payments, dividend payments, and proceeds from the sale of any financial instrument, shall be paid into the general fund of the Treasury for reduction of the public debt."[42]

THE SENATE-PASSED VERSION OF THE SBLF

Title IV of the Senate-passed version of H.R. 5297, which later became law, authorized the Secretary of the Treasury to establish a $30 billion SBLF to make capital investments in eligible community banks with total assets equal to or less than $1 billion or $10 billion. There were several differences between the Senate-passed version of H.R. 5297's SBLF provisions and the SBLF provisions in the House-passed version of H.R. 5297. Specifically,

- the House-passed version of H.R. 5297 indicated that eligible institutions may be insured depository institutions that are not controlled by a bank holding company or a savings and loan holding company that is also an eligible institution and is not directly or indirectly controlled by any company or other entity that has total consolidated assets of more than $10 billion, bank holding companies, savings and loan holding companies, community development financial institution loan funds, and small business lending companies, all with total assets of $10 billion or less (as of the end of 2009).[43] The Senate-passed version of H.R. 5297 did not provide eligibility to small business lending companies.[44]
- the House-passed version of H.R. 5297 defined small business lending "as small business lending as defined by and reported in an eligible institution's quarterly call report, where each loan comprising such lending is made to a small business and is one the following types: (1) commercial and industrial loans; (2) owner-occupied nonfarm, nonresidential real estate loans; (3) loans to finance agricultural production and other loans to farmers; (4) loans secured by farmland; (5) nonowner-occupied commercial real estate loans; and (6) construction, land development and other land loans."[45] The Senate-passed version of H.R. 5297's definition of small business lending did not include nonowner-occupied commercial real estate or construction, land development and other land loans.[46]
- the Senate-passed version of H.R. 5297 had an exclusion provision prohibiting recipient lending institutions from using the funds to issue loans that have an original amount greater than $10 million or that would be made to a business with more than $50 million in revenues.[47] The House-passed version of H.R. 5297 did not contain this provision.
- the House-passed version of H.R. 5297 indicated that the incentives received in the form of reduced dividend rates during the first 4.5-year period following the date on which an eligible institution received a capital investment under the program would be contingent on an

increase in the number of loans made.[48] If the number of loans made by the institution did not increase by 2.5% for each 2.5% increase of small business lending, then the rate at which dividends and interest would be payable during the following quarter on preferred stock or other financial instruments issued to the Treasury by the eligible institution would be (i) 5%, if this quarter is within the two-year period following the date on which the eligible institution received the capital investment under the program; or (ii) 7%, if the quarter is after the two-year period. The Senate-passed version of H.R. 5297 did not contain this legislative language.

- the House-passed version of H.R. 5297 included an alternative computation provision that would have allowed eligible institutions to compute their small business lending amounts for incentive purposes as if the definition of their small business lending amounts did not require that the loans comprising such lending be made to small business.[49] This alternative computation would have been allowed if the eligible institution certified that all lending included by the institution for purposes of computing the increase in lending was made to small businesses. The Senate-passed version of H.R. 5297 did not contain this provision.
- the House-passed version of H.R. 5297 indicated that an eligible institution that is a community development loan fund may apply to receive a capital investment from the SBLF in an amount not exceeding 10% of total assets, as reported in the audited financial statements for the fiscal year of the eligible institution that ended in calendar year 2009.[50] The Senate-passed version of H.R. 5297 specifies 5%.[51]
- the House-passed version of H.R. 5297 would have required the Secretary of the Treasury, in consultation with the Community Development Financial Institutions Fund, to develop eligibility criteria to determine the financial ability of a Community Development Loan Fund to participate in the program and repay the investment. It provided a list of recommended eligibility criteria that the Secretary of the Treasury could use for this purpose.[52] The Senate-passed version of H.R. 5297 provided a similar, but mandatory, list of eligibility criteria that must be used for this purpose.[53]
- the House-passed version of H.R. 5297 contained a temporary amortization authority provision which would have allowed an

eligible institution to amortize any loss or write-down on a quarterly straight-line basis over a period of time, adjusted to reflect the institution's change in the amount of small business lending relative to the baseline.[54] The Senate-passed version of H.R. 5297 did not contain this provision.

The Senate's version of H.R. 5297 was agreed to in the Senate on September 16, 2010, after considerable debate and amendment to remove the Small Business Early-Stage Investment Program and Small Business Borrower Assistance Program, revise the SBLF, and add numerous other provisions to assist small businesses, including additional small business tax reduction provisions.[55] The House agreed to the Senate amendments on September 23, 2010, and President Obama signed the bill, renamed the Small Business Jobs Act of 2010 (P.L. 111-240), into law on September 27, 2010.

ARGUMENTS FOR AND AGAINST THE SBLF

The SBLF's advocates argued that it would create jobs by encouraging lenders, especially those experiencing liquidity problems (access to cash and easily tradable assets),[56] to increase their lending to small businesses. For example, the House report accompanying H.R. 5297 argued that the SBLF was needed to enhance small business's access to capital, which, in turn, was necessary to enable those businesses to create jobs and assist in the economic recovery:

> There has been a dramatic decrease in the amount of bank lending in the past several quarters. On May 20, 2010, the Federal Deposit Insurance Corporation (FDIC) released its Quarterly Banking Profile for the first quarter of 2010. The report shows that commercial and industrial loans declined for the seventh straight quarter, down more than 17% from the year before.
>
> Many companies, particularly small businesses, claim that it is becoming harder to get new loans to keep their business operating and that banks are tightening requirements or cutting off existing lines of credit even when the businesses are up to date on their loan repayments. Treasury Secretary Timothy F. Geithner recently acknowledged the problem encountered by some banks, both healthy and troubled, which have been

> told to maintain capital levels in excess of those required to be considered well capitalized.
>
> Some banks say they have little choice but to scale back lending, even to creditworthy borrowers, and the most recent Federal Reserve data shows banks are continuing to tighten lending terms for small businesses.[57]

A dissenting view, endorsed by the House Committee on Financial Services' minority members, was included in the report. They argued that the SBLF does not properly deal with the lack of financing for small businesses:

> Instead of addressing the problem by stimulating demand for credit by small businesses, H.R. 5297 injects capital into banks with no guarantees that they will actually lend. The bill allows a qualifying bank to obtain a capital infusion from the government without even requiring the bank to make a loan for two years. In fact, if a bank reduces or fails to increase lending to small business during those first two years, it would not face any penalty. It defies logic that the Majority would support a bill to increase lending that does not actually require increased lending. A more effective response to the challenges facing America's small businesses was offered by Representatives Biggert, Paulsen, Castle, Gerlach, and King, whose amendment would have extended a series of small business tax credits before implementing the Small Business Lending Fund.[58]

They also argued that even if the SBLF was authorized "the program probably would not be fully operational for months; banks could shun the program for fear of being stigmatized by its association with TARP; and many banks would avoid taking on new liabilities when their existing assets are troubled."[59] They also argued that the bill did not provide sufficient oversight for effectively monitoring the program because the Inspector General of the Department of the Treasury, who was given that responsibility under the bill, "might not be able to direct sufficient attention to this task given its other responsibilities."[60] They argued that the Special Inspector General of TARP would be in a better position to provide effective oversight of the program.[61]

These, and other, arguments were presented during House floor debate on the bill. For example, Representative Melissa Bean advocated the bill's passage, arguing that the SBLF

> builds on the effective financial stabilization measures Congress has previously taken by establishing a new $30 billion small business loan fund to provide additional capital to community banks that increase

> lending to small businesses. This $30 billion investment on which the government will be collecting dividends and earning a profit per the CBO estimates can be leveraged by banks into over $300 billion in new small business loans. This is an important investment by the Federal Government in our small business that brings tremendous returns.
>
> The terms of the capital provided to banks are performance based; the more a bank increases its small business lending, the lower the dividend rate is for the SBLF capital. If a bank decreases its small business lending, it will be penalized with higher dividend rates.
>
> This legislation includes strong safeguards to ensure that banks adequately utilize available funds to increase lending to small businesses, not for other lending or to improve their balance sheet. There will be oversight consistently throughout the program, plus it requires that the capital be invested only in strong financial institutions at little risk of default and the best positioned to increase small business lending.
>
> It's important for Americans to understand that although this fund has a maximum value of $30 billion, it is estimated to make a profit for taxpayers in the long run. And the money will ultimately go not to banks, but to the small businesses and their communities that they lend to. As our financial system stabilizes and our community banks recapitalize, these funds will be repaid to Treasury with full repayment required over the next 10 years.[62]

Representative Nydia Velázquez, then the chair of the House Committee on Small Business, added that the legislation had sufficient safeguards in place to ensure that the funds were targeted at small businesses:

> First, banks must apply to the Treasury to receive funds, with a detailed plan on how to increase small business lending at their institution. This language was included at my insistence that we need to make sure that small businesses will get the benefit of this legislation.
>
> Second, this capital, repayment of the government loans will be at a dividend rate starting at 5% per year. This rate will be lowered by 1% for every 2.5% increase in small business lending over 2009 levels. It can go as low as a total dividend rate of just 1% if the bank increases its business lending by 10% or more, incentivizing banks to do the right thing. To ensure that banks actually use the funding they receive, the rate will increase—and there are penalties—to 7% if the bank fails to increase its small business lending at their institution within 2 years. To ensure that all federal funds are paid back within 5 years, the dividend rate will

increase to 9% for all banks, irrespective of their small business lending, after 4 1/2 years.[63]

Representative Velázquez added "let me just make it clear ... CBO estimates that [the SBLF] will save taxpayers $1 billion over 10 years, as banks are expected to pay back this loan over 10 years, with interest."[64]

Representative Randy Neugebauer opposed the bill's adoption, arguing that

> the majority is repeating the same failed initiatives that have helped our national debt grow to $13 trillion in the past 2 years. This bill follows the model of the TARP program, minus [TARP's] stronger oversight, and it puts another $30 billion into banks in the hopes that lending to small businesses will increase. In the words of Neil Barofsky, the Special Inspector General who oversees the TARP, "In terms of its basic design," he says, "its participants, its application process, from an oversight perspective, the Small Business Lending Fund would essentially be an extension of the TARP's Capital Purchase Program." From the Congressional Oversight Panel for TARP, chaired by Elizabeth Warren, she says, "The SBLF's prospects are far from certain. The SBLF also raises questions about whether, in light of the Capital Purchase Program's poor performance in improving credit access, any capital infusion program can successfully jump-start small business lending."
>
> This bill allows for another $33 billion in spending that will be added to the government's credit card. The CBO tells us that the bank lending portion will ultimately cost taxpayers $3.4 billion when market risk is taken into account.[65]

The arguments presented during House floor debate on H.R. 5297 were also presented during Senate consideration of the bill. Advocates argued that the SBLF would encourage higher levels of small business lending and jobs. For example, Senator Mary Landrieu argued on July 21, 2010, that the SBLF should be adopted because it "is not a government program for banks. It is a public-private partnership lending strategy for small business."[66] She added that as chair of the Senate Committee on Small Business and Entrepreneurship she talked with her colleagues, including the SBLF's opponents, and revised the program to address their concerns. She also argued that the SBLF has

> hundreds of endorsements from independent banks, the community banks and almost every small business association in America ... makes $1

> billion [according to the CBO score] ... is not direct lending from the federal government. It is not creating a new bureaucracy ... [It is] voluntary ... there are no onerous restrictions.... The small business gets the loans. We create jobs. People are employed. The recession starts ending.... It has nothing to do with TARP money. It is not a TARP program. It is not a bank program. It doesn't have anything to do with banks except that we are working in partnership with banks to lend money to small businesses which are desperate for money.[67]

Opponents argued that the SBLF could lose money, lacked sufficient oversight provisions, did not require lenders to increase their lending to small businesses, could serve as a vehicle for TARP recipients to effectively refinance their TARP loans on more favorable terms with little or any resulting benefit for small businesses, and could encourage a failing lender to make even riskier loans to avoid higher dividend payments. In addition, there were disagreements over the number of amendments that could be offered by the minority, which led several Senators to oppose further consideration of the bill until that issue was resolved to their satisfaction. For example, on July 22, 2010, Senator Olympia Snowe argued that although "under a cash-based estimate, CBO listed the official score for the lending fund as raising $1.1 billion over 10 years," SBLF proponents "fail to mention" that when CBO scored the SBLF using an alternative methodology that adjusts for market risk, it estimated that the SBLF could cost $6.2 billion.[68] Senator Snowe also argued that the bipartisan Congressional Oversight Panel for TARP stated in its May 2010 oversight report that the proposed SBLF "substantially resembles" the TARP program and "is a bank-focused capital infusion program that is being contemplated despite little, if any, evidence that such programs increase lending."[69] Senator Snowe also stated that she regretted "that we are in a position where we have not been able to reach agreement allowing the minority to offer amendments, which is confounding and perplexing as well as disappointing."[70] Senator Snowe later added that the SBLF's incentives to encourage lending to small businesses also "could encourage unnecessarily risky behavior by banks ... to avoid paying higher interest rates."[71]

Opponents also questioned the SBLF's use of quarterly call report data as submitted by lenders to their appropriate banking regulator to determine what counts as a small business loan.[72] Call report data denotes loans of $1 million or less as small business loans, regardless of the size of the business receiving the loan. As a result, the SBLF's opponents argued that "the data used to measure small business lending in the SBLF covers an entirely different set of small businesses than those that fall within the definition set out in the Small Business Act or used by the SBA."[73]

As mentioned previously, the Senate's version of H.R. 5297 was agreed to on September 16, 2010, by a vote of 68-38.[74] The House agreed to the Senate-passed version of H.R. 5297 on September 23, 2010, by a vote of 237-187, and the bill was signed into law by President Obama on September 27, 2010.

THE SBLF'S IMPLEMENTATION

On February 14, 2011, the Obama Administration issued its budget recommendation for FY2012. It anticipated that the SBLF would provide $17.399 billion in financings, well below its authorized amount of $30 billion.[75] This was the first indication that the SBLF's implementation may not proceed as expected.[76] The second indication that the program's implementation may not proceed as expected was an unanticipated delay in the writing of the program's regulations.

Treasury's Roll Out of the Program

The U.S. Treasury was criticized by some for not implementing the program quickly enough.[77] The first financing took place on June 21, 2011, about nine months after the program's enactment. The delay was largely due to the Treasury's need to finalize the SBLF's investment decision process with federal banking agencies[78] and the need to create separate SBLF regulations for financial institutions established as C Corporations, Subchapter S Corporations, mutual lending institutions, and community development financial institutions (CDFIs).

A "C corporation" is a legal entity established under state law and includes shareholders, directors, and officers. The profit of a C corporation is taxed to the corporation when earned, and then is taxed to the shareholders when distributed as dividends.[79] The majority of insured depository institutions, bank holding companies, and savings and loan holding companies are C corporations.[80] A "Subchapter S Corporation" refers to a section of the Internal Revenue Code (IRS) that allows a corporation to pass corporate income, losses, deductions, and credits through to their shareholders for federal tax purposes. Shareholders of S corporations report the flow-through of income and losses on their personal tax returns and are assessed tax at their individual income tax rates. This allows S corporations to avoid double taxation on the corporate income.[81] Mutual lending institutions, which include many thrifts and savings and loans associations, are owned by its depositors or policyholders. They have no stockholders. CDFIs are financial entities certified by the Community Development Financial Institutions Fund (CDFI Fund) in the U.S Department of the Treasury, and provide capital and financial services to underserved communities.

The establishment of separate regulations for each of these different types of financial institutions was largely related to issues involving whether the SBLF's financings would be counted by banking regulatory agencies as Tier 1 capital (core capital that is relatively liquid, such as common shareholders' equity, disclosed reserves, most retained earnings, and perpetual non-cumulative preferred stocks) or as Tier 2 capital (supplementary capital that consists mainly of undisclosed reserves, revaluation reserves, general provisions, hybrid instruments and subordinated term debt).[82]

The treatment of the SBLF's financings was important given that banks must maintain a minimum total risk-based capital ratio of 8% (the ratio measures bank capital against assets, with asset values risk-weighted, or adjusted on a scale of riskiness) to be considered adequately capitalized by federal banking regulators. In addition, banks must maintain a minimum Tier 1 risk-based ratio to assets, typically 3% for banking institutions with the highest financial ratings and 4% for others.[83]

According to Treasury officials, under Internal Revenue Service (IRS) rules, S corporations can have only a single class of stock (common shares). Consequently, these institutions cannot issue preferred stock to Treasury. As a result, Treasury had to consider purchasing subordinated debt from these institutions, which the banking regulatory agencies would likely designate as Tier 2 capital.[84] Treasury officials believed that providing Tier 2 capital would probably result in fewer S corporation participants. Additionally, because mutual institutions do not issue stock, Treasury officials were unable to receive preferred stock as consideration for an investment in this type of institution. Therefore, Treasury had to consider purchasing subordinated debt from these institutions as well.[85]

Treasury completed its regulations for C corporation banks first. For C Corporations, SBLF funds will be treated as Tier I capital and the Treasury will purchase senior perpetual noncumulative preferred stock (or an equivalent). The stock will pay a quarterly dividend on the first day of each quarter after closing of the SBLF capital program funding. Tier 1 capital is the core measure of a bank's financial strength from a regulator's point of view. It is composed of core capital, which consists primarily of common stock and disclosed reserves (or retained earnings), but may also include non-redeemable non-cumulative preferred stock. In contrast, S Corporations and mutual lending institutions will receive unsecured subordinated debentures from the Treasury, which will be considered Tier 2 capital for regulatory capital requirements.[86]

The application deadline for C corporation banks was May 16, 2011. The application deadline for Subchapter S corporations and mutual lending institutions was June 6, 2011, and the application deadline for CDFIs was June 22, 2011. A total of 926 institutions applied for $11.8 billion in SBLF funding.[87]

Treasury approved $4,027,703,880 in SBLF financing to 332 lending institutions.[88] SBLF recipients have offices located in 47 states and the District of Columbia. The average financing was $12,131,638, ranging from $42,000 to $141,000,000.[89]

Of the 332 lending institutions which received financing, 137 institutions had participated in TARP's Community Development Capital Initiative or its Capital Purchase Program. These institutions received $2,689,763,790 in SBLF financing (66.8% of the total).[90]

Small Business Lending Progress Reports

Treasury is required to publish monthly reports describing all of the transactions made under the SBLF program during the reporting period. It is also required to publish a semiannual report (each March and September) providing all projected costs and liabilities, all operating expenses, and all transactions made by the SBLF, including a list of all participating institutions and the amounts each institution has received under the program. Treasury is also required to publish a quarterly report describing how participating institutions have used the funds they have received under the program.[91]

Institutions participating in the SBLF are required to submit an Initial Supplemental Report to Treasury, no later than five business days before closing. It provides information from the institution's FDIC call reports or, for holding companies, from their subsidiaries' FDIC call reports, that Treasury uses to establish an initial baseline for measuring the SBLF participants' progress in making loans to small businesses.[92]

The initial baseline small business lending amount is the average amount of qualified small business lending that was outstanding for the four-full quarters ending on June 30, 2010.[93] This initial baseline amount is derived by first adding the outstanding amount of lending reported for all commercial and industrial loans, owner-occupied nonfarm, nonresidential real estate loans, loans to finance agricultural production and other loans to farmers, and loans secured by farmland. Then, the outstanding amount of lending for large loans (defined as any loan or group of loans greater than $10 million), loans to large businesses (defined as businesses with annual revenues greater than $50 million), and the portion of any loans guaranteed by the U.S. government or for which the risk is assumed by a third party is subtracted from that amount. The lending institution then adds back any cumulative charge-offs with respect to such loans since July 1, 2010. This last adjustment is done to prevent lending institutions from being penalized for appropriately charging off loans.[94]

According to the Initial Supplemental Reports submitted by the SBLF's participants, the baseline level of small business lending for future comparisons is $35.9 billion.[95] This initial baseline amount is expected to remain fairly constant. However, it will be adjusted to take into account any gains in qualified small business lending during the four baseline quarters resulting from mergers, acquisitions, and loan purchases by the SBLF's participants. This adjustment is designed to ensure that future dividend rate reductions provided to any SBLF participant corresponds to additional lending to small businesses and not to the acquisition of existing loans.[96]

SBLF institutions are also required to submit Quarterly Supplemental Reports, due in the calendar quarter following submission of the Initial Supplemental Report and in each of the next nine quarters, to determine their dividend rate for the next quarter.[97]

Using information contained in the Quarterly Supplemental Reports, Treasury announced in its quarterly "Use of Funds" report released on January 9, 2012, that, as of September 30, 2011,

> institutions participating in SBLF have made important progress in increasing their small business lending, helping to support small businesses and local economies across the nation:
>
> - In total, SBLF participants have increased their small business lending by $3.5 billion over a $35.9 billion baseline.

- Increases in small business lending are widespread across SBLF participants, with 78% of participants [259 of 332] having already increased their small business lending over baseline levels.
- A substantial majority of SBLF participants—more than 60% of participants [203 of 332] —have now increased their small business lending by 10% or more.[98]

On January 10, 2012, Donald Graves, Deputy Assistant Secretary at Treasury, announced that the Quarterly Use of Funds report released the previous day "contains strong evidence that the Small Business Lending Fund is working."[99] He added that "this report on SBLF is encouraging, and we look forward to even stronger reports in the future."[100]

Some financial commentators had a somewhat less sanguine view of the report's findings. For example, one commentator noted that while the report of increased small business lending was positive news "it is difficult to isolate the proportion of new lending that would have occurred anyway" due to improvements in the economy.[101] Another commentator noted that the data may have been skewed by SBLF participants who were entering the small business lending market for the first time, making the increases appear larger and more significant than they actually are; another noted that the reported growth in small business lending occurred over six quarters (since June 30, 2010) and that the results, while positive, are "not as impressive as it may seem."[102]

PROPOSED LEGISLATION

Several bills have been introduced in the 112th Congress to amend the SBLF. For example, Senator Snowe introduced S. 681, the Greater Accountability in the Lending Fund Act of 2011, on March 30, 2011. Senator Snowe argued that

> While I would prefer to terminate this fund altogether, it is unlikely based on the current political environment, which is why we must work to protect taxpayers from some of its most egregious provisions. My goal with this legislation is to ensure that only healthy banks have access to taxpayer money, that they are required to repay loans within a reasonable period of time, and that small businesses find the affordable credit they need.[103]

The bill would, among other things,

- require recipients to repay SBLF distributions within 10 years of the receipt of the investment,[104]
- terminate the program no later than 15 years after the date of the bill's enactment,[105]
- prohibit the Secretary of the Treasury from making capital investments under the program if the FDIC is appointed receiver of 5% or more of the institutions receiving an investment under the program,
- prohibit participation by any institution that received an investment under TARP (effective on the date of the bill's enactment),
- remove provisions allowing the Secretary of Treasury to make a capital investment in institutions that would otherwise not be recommended to receive the investment based on the institution's financial condition, but are able to provide a matching investment from private, nongovernmental investors,
- require the approval of appropriate financial regulators when determining whether an institution should receive a capital investment,[106] and
- revise the benchmark against which changes in the amount of small business lending is measured from the four full quarters immediately preceding the date of enactment to calendar year 2007.[107]

Representative Patrick McHenry introduced H.R. 1387, the Small Business Lending Fund Accountability Act of 2011, on May 2, 2011. It would give the Special Inspector General for TARP responsibility for providing oversight over the SBLF.

Senator Tom Coburn proposed S.Amdt. 279 to S. 493, the Small Business Innovation Research, Small Business Technology Transfer Reauthorization Act of 2011, on March 31, 2011. It would prevent TARP recipients from using funds received in any form under any other federal assistance program, including the SBLF program.

Representative Cedric Richmond, introduced H.R. 2807, the Small Business Leg-Up Act of 2011, on August 5, 2011. It would transfer any unobligated and repaid funds from the SBLF to the Community Development Financial Institutions Fund beginning on the date when the Secretary of the Treasury's authority to make capital investments in eligible institutions expires (on September 27, 2011). The bill's stated intent is "to increase the availability of credit for small businesses."[108]

Representative John Carney introduced H.R. 3147, the Small Business Lending Extension Act, on October 21, 2011. It would extend the Treasury Department's investment authority from one year following enactment to two years and require the Treasury Secretary to provide any institution not selected for participation in the program the reason for the rejection, ensure that the rejection reason remains confidential, and establish an appeal process that provides the institution an opportunity to contest the reason provided for the rejection of its application.

CONCLUDING OBSERVATIONS

The SBLF was enacted as part of a larger effort to enhance the supply of capital to small businesses. Advocates argued that the SBLF would help to address the recent decline in small business lending and create jobs. Opponents were not convinced that it would enhance small business lending, and worried about the program's potential cost to the federal treasury and its similarities to TARP.

It is still too early to determine the extent of the program's affect on small business lending. Under the Small Business Jobs Act, the Department of the Treasury's Inspector General is required to conduct audits and investigations of the SBLF and to report its findings to Congress and the Secretary of the Treasury no less than two times a year. To date, Treasury's Inspector General has released two semiannual audits, the first on May 13, 2011, and the second on December 22, 2011.[109] The first audit focused on Treasury's investment decision process for evaluating SBLF applicants. The second audit focused on Treasury's cost and liabilities projections for the program. In addition, the Government Accountability Office is required to audit the program annually.[110]

Although not specifically mandated by law, these audits could address the program's affect on small business lending.[111] However, any analysis of the program's influence on small business lending is likely to be more suggestive than definitive because differentiating the SBLF's affect on small business lending from other factors, such as changes in the lender's local economy, is methodologically challenging, especially given the relatively small amount of financing involved relative to the national market for small business loans. The

SBLF's $4.0 billion in financing represents less than 0.6% of outstanding small business loans.

It is also too early to fully address opponents' concerns about the program's potential cost. In December 2010, before accepting any applicants, Treasury initially estimated that the SBLF could cost taxpayers up to $1.26 billion (excluding administrative costs that are an estimated $26 million annually).[112]

It based that estimate with an expectation that about $17 billion in SBLF financings would be disbursed. In October 2011, Treasury estimated the program's costs based on actual participant data. It estimated that the SBLF will generate a savings of $0.08 billion, with the savings coming primarily from a lower than expected financing level and, to a lesser extent, improvements in projected default rates "due to higher participant quality than expected" and lower market interest rates.[113]

One issue that has arisen relative to the program's projected cost is the non-cumulative treatment of dividends. The Treasury's Inspector General reported in May 2011 that

> Under the terms set by legislation, dividend payments are non-cumulative, meaning that institutions are under no obligation to make dividend payments as scheduled or to pay off previously missed payments before exiting the program. This dividend treatment differs from the TARP programs, in which many dividend payments were cumulative. This change in dividend treatment was driven by changes in capital requirements mandated by the Collins Amendment to the Dodd-Frank Act.
>
> The amendment equalizes the consolidated capital requirements for Tier 1 capital of bank holding companies by requiring that, at a minimum, regulators apply the same capital and risk standards for FDIC-insured banks to bank holding companies. Under TARP, the FRB [Federal Reserve Board] and FDIC treated capital differently at the holding company and depository institution levels. The FRB treated cumulative securities issued by holding companies as Tier 1 capital, while FDIC treated non-cumulative securities issued by depository institutions as Tier 1 capital. In order to comply with the Dodd-Frank Act requirement that securities purchased from holding companies receive the same capital treatment as those purchased from depository institutions, Treasury made the dividends under SBLF non-cumulative.

Additionally, given that Tier 1 capital must be perpetual and cannot have a mandatory redemption date, the 10-year repayment period in the Small Business Jobs Act cannot be enforced.[114]

Treasury has addressed this issue by placing the following additional requirements and restrictions on participants who miss dividend payments:

- the participant's CEO [Chief Executive Office] and CFO [Chief Financial Officer] must provide written notice regarding the rationale of the board of directors (BOD) for not declaring a dividend,
- no repurchases may be affected and no dividends may be declared on any securities for the applicable quarter and the following three quarters,
- after four missed payments (consecutive or not), the issuer's BOD must certify in writing that the issuer used best efforts to declare and pay dividends appropriately,
- after five missed payments (consecutive or not), Treasury may appoint a representative to serve as an observer on the issuer's BOD, and
- after six missed payments (consecutive or not), Treasury may elect two directors to the issuer's BOD if the liquidation preference is $25 million or more.[115]

The Treasury's Inspector General agreed that Treasury's equity investment policy is consistent with the legislation and that "it has reasonably structured the program to incentivize payment of dividends."[116] However, it recommended that "Congress consider whether an amendment to the Small Business Jobs Act and/or waiver from the Collins Amendment to the Dodd-Frank Act is needed to make the repayment of dividends a requirement for exiting the program."[117]

In conclusion, congressional oversight of the SBLF is currently focused on the program's potential long-term costs and affect on small business lending.

Underlying those concerns are fundamental disagreements concerning the best way to assist small businesses. Some advocate the provision of additional federal resources to assist small businesses in acquiring capital necessary to start, continue, or expand operations and create jobs. Others worry about the longterm adverse economic effects of spending programs that increase the federal deficit.

They advocate business tax reduction, reform of financial credit market regulation, and federal fiscal restraint as the best means to assist small businesses and create jobs.

End Notes

[1] The United States does not have a statutory definition for medium-sized businesses and a business concern can either be considered "small" or not small under section 3(a)(1) of the Small Business Act, 15 U.S.C. § 632(a)(1), which indicates that a small business concern "shall be deemed to be one that is independently owned and operated and which is not dominant in its field of operation." The act authorizes the SBA's Administrator to define small business size standards based on industry classifications and the SBA has denominated 42 separate size standards covering 1,158 business classifications which may be found at 13 C.F.R. §121.201. A statistical analysis of the SBA's size standards database reveals that the median size of small business is 500 employees. In contrast, the European Union defines small business as those with fewer than 50 employees, medium-sized business as those employing between 50 to 500 workers, and large businesses as those with over 500 employees. Under the SBA size standards a small business concern can have up to 1,500 employees for certain industry categories. For additional information and analysis see CRS Report R40860, Defining Small Business: A Historical Analysis of Contemporary Issues, by Robert Jay Dilger.

[2] U.S. Small Business Administration, Office of Advocacy, "Small Business Economic Indicators for 2003: A reference guide to the latest data on small business activity, including state and industry data," Washington, DC, August 2004, p. 3, http://archive.sba.gov/advo /stats/sbei03.pdf; and Brian Headd, "Small Businesses Most Likely to Lead Economic Recovery," The Small Business Advocate, vol. 28, no. 6 (July 2009), pp. 1, 2.

[3] U.S. Small Business Administration, Office of Advocacy, "Small Business Economic Indicators for 2003: A reference guide to the latest data on small business activity, including state and industry data," Washington, DC, August 2004, p. 3, http://archive.sba .gov/ advo / stats /sbei03.pdf.

[4] Ibid.

[5] U.S. Small Business Administration, "The Small Business Economy, 2010: A Report to the President," Washington, DC, 2010, pp. 2, 5, 21, 22, http://www.sba.gov/sites/default/ files /sb_econ2010.pdf; and U.S. Small Business Administration, Fiscal Year 2010 Congressional Budget Justification (Washington, DC: GPO, 2009), p. 1, http://www.sba. gov/sites/default/files/Congressional_Budget_Justification_2010.pdf.

[6] U.S. Small Business Administration, Office of Advocacy, "Small Business Quarterly Bulletin: Second Quarter 2011," Washington, DC, http://www.sba.gov/sites/ default/files/ files/SBQB_2011q2.pdf; and U.S. Small Business Administration, Office of Advocacy, "Small Business Quarterly Bulletin: Third Quarter 2011," Washington, DC, http://www. sba.gov/sites/default/files/SBQB_2011q3.pdf.

[7] U.S. Small Business Administration, Office of Advocacy, "Small Business Quarterly Bulletin: Second Quarter 2011," Washington, DC, http://www.sba.gov/sites/default/files/ files/ SBQB_2011q2.pdf; and U.S. Small Business Administration, Office of Advocacy, "Small

Business Quarterly Bulletin: Third Quarter 2011," Washington, DC, http://www.sba.gov/sites/default/files/SBQB_2011q3.pdf.

[8] Federal Deposit Insurance Corporation, "Statistics on Depository Institutions," http:// www 2. fdic.gov/SDI/main.asp.

[9] Ibid.

[10] U.S. Small Business Administration, "Jobs Act Supported More Than $12 Billion in SBA Lending to Small Businesses in Just Three Months," Washington, DC, January 3, 2010, http://www.sba.gov/content/jobs-act-supportedmore-12-billion-sba-lending-small-businesses-just-three-months.

[11] H.R. 2807, the Small Business Leg-Up Act of 2011.

[12] Federal Reserve Board, "Senior Loan Officer Opinion Survey on Bank Lending Practices," Washington, DC, http://www.federalreserve.gov/boarddocs/SnLoanSurvey/; and Brian Headd, "Forum Seeks Solutions To Thaw Frozen Small Business Credit," The Small Business Advocate, vol. 28, no. 10 (December 2009), p. 3, http://www.sba.gov/sites/default/files/The%20Small%20Business%20Advocate%20-%20December%202009.pdf.

[13] Federal Reserve Board, "The April 2010 Senior Loan Officer Opinion Survey on Bank Lending Practices," Washington, DC, http://www.federalreserve.gov/boarddocs/Sn Loan Survey/201005/default.htm.

[14] Federal Reserve Board, "Senior Loan Officer Opinion Survey on Bank Lending Practices," Washington, DC, http://www.federalreserve.gov/boarddocs/SnLoanSurvey/.

[15] George W. Haynes and Victoria Williams, Lending by Depository Lenders to Small Businesses, 2003 to 2010, U.S. Small Business Administration, Office of Advocacy, Washington, DC, March 2011, http://www.sba.gov/sites/default/ files/rs380tot.pdf.

[16] Ibid., p. 25.

[17] Ibid., p. 26. One possible contributing factor for at least some lenders becoming more cautious is that in recent years many lenders experienced an increase in non-performing loans and a depletion of their loan loss reserves, limiting the funds available for lending to small businesses.

[18] Ibid., p. 26.

[19] Ibid., p. 25.

[20] Ibid.

[21] William C. Dunkelberg and Holly Wade, Small Business Economic Trends (Washington, DC: NFIB Research Foundation, September 2011), p. 18, http://www.nfib.com/ Portals/0/PDF/sbet/sbet201109.pdf; and William J. Dennis, Jr., Small Business Credit in a Deep Recession (Washington, DC: NFIB Research Foundation, June 2008), p. 1, http://www.nfib.com/LinkClick.aspx?fileticket=IPeviHUzXfE%3D&tabid=90&mid=3121.

[22] U.S. Small Business Administration, "The Small Business Economy, 2010: A Report to the President," Washington, DC, 2010, pp. 2, 5, 21, 22, http://www.sba.gov/ sites/default /files/sb_econ2010.pdf; and U.S. Small Business Administration, Fiscal Year 2010 Congressional Budget Justification (Washington, DC: GPO, 2009), p. 1, http://www.sba.gov/sites/default/files/ Congressional_Budget_ ustification_2010.pdf.

[23] U.S. Congress, House Committee on Small Business, The State of Small Business Access to Capital and Credit: The View from Secretary Geithner, 112th Cong., 1st sess., June 22, 2011, p. 1.

[24] U.S. Small Business Administration, Office of Advocacy, "Small Business Quarterly Bulletin: Second Quarter 2011," Washington, DC, http://www.sba.gov/sites/default/files/files/SBQB_2011q2.pdf; and U.S. Small Business Administration, Office of Advocacy, "Small

Business Quarterly Bulletin: Third Quarter 2011," Washington, DC, http://www.sba.gov/sites/default/files/SBQB_2011q3.pdf.

25 P.L. 111-5, the American Recovery and Reinvestment Act of 2009, provided the SBA $375 million to subsidize fees for the SBA's 7(a) and 504/CDC loan guaranty programs and to increase the 7(a) program's maximum loan guaranty percentage from up to 85% of loans of $150,000 or less and up to 75% of loans exceeding $150,000 to 90% for all regular 7(a) loans through September 30, 2010, or when appropriated funding for the subsidies and loan modification was exhausted. P.L. 111-118, the Department of Defense Appropriations Act, 2010, provided the SBA $125 million to continue the fee subsides and 90% maximum loan guaranty percentage through February 28, 2010. P.L. 111-144, the Temporary Extension Act of 2010, provided the SBA $60 million to continue the fee subsides and 90% maximum loan guaranty percentage through March 28, 2010. P.L. 111-150, an act to extend the Small Business Loan Guarantee Program, and for other purposes, provided the SBA authority to reprogram $40 million in previously appropriated funds to continue the fee subsides and 90% maximum loan guaranty percentage through April 30, 2010. P.L. 111-157, the Continuing Extension Act of 2010, provided the SBA $80 million to continue the SBA's fee subsides and 90% maximum loan guaranty percentage through May 31, 2010. P.L. 111-240, the Small Business Jobs Act of 2010, provided $505 million (plus an additional $5 million for administrative expenses) to continue the SBA's fee subsides and 90% maximum loan guaranty percentage from the act's date of enactment (September 27, 2010) through December 31, 2010. P.L. 111-322, the Continuing Appropriations and Surface Transportation Extensions Act, 2011, authorizes the SBA to use funds provided under the Small Business Jobs Act of 2010 to continue the SBA's fee subsides and 90% maximum loan guaranty percentage through March 4, 2011, or until available funding is exhausted—which occurred on January 3, 2011.

26 P.L. 111-5, the American Recovery and Reinvestment Act of 2009, Sec. 505, Increasing Small Business Investment.

27 Ibid.

28 U.S. Small Business Administration, Office of Congressional and Legislative Affairs, correspondence with the author, Washington, DC, January 4, 2010.

29 The act also temporarily allows the SBA to waive, in whole or in part, for successive fiscal years, the non-federal share requirement for loans to the Microloan program's intermediaries and for grants made to Microloan intermediaries for small business marketing, management, and technical assistance under specified circumstances (e.g., the economic conditions affecting the intermediary). See P.L. 111-240, the Small Business Jobs Act of 2010, Sec. 1401. Matching Requirements Under Small Business Programs.

30 P.L. 110-343, the Emergency Economic Stabilization Act of 2008, was designed to enhance the supply of loans to businesses of all sizes. The act authorized the Troubled Asset Relief Program (TARP) to "restore liquidity and stability to the financial system of the United States" by purchasing or insuring up to $700 billion in troubled assets from banks and other financial institutions. TARP's purchase authority was later reduced from $700 billion to $475 billion by P.L. 111-203, the Dodd-Frank Wall Street Reform and Consumer Protection Act. The Department of the Treasury has disbursed $389 billion in TARP funds, including $337 million to purchase SBA 7(a) loan guaranty program securities. The authority to make new TARP commitments expired on October 3, 2010. U.S. Department of the Treasury, Troubled Assets Relief Program Monthly 105(a) Report—November 2010, Washington, DC, December 10, 2010, pp. 2-4, http://www.financialstability.gov /docs/ November%

20105(a)%20FINAL.pdf. For further analysis see CRS Report R41427, Troubled Asset Relief Program (TARP): Implementation and Status, by Baird Webel.

[31] The White House, "Remarks by the President to Small Business Owners, Community Leaders, and Members of Congress," March 16, 2009, http://www.whitehouse.gov /the_ press_office/Remarks-by-the-President-to-small-businessowners/.

[32] Emily Flitter, "Fix for SBA Snagged by Tarp's Exec Comp Limits," American Banker, vol. 174, no. 61 (March 31, 2009), p. 1.

33 The White House, "Remarks by the President in State of the Union Address," January 27, 2010, http://www.whitehouse.gov/the-press-office/remarks-president-state-union-address.

34 The White House, "President Obama Outlines New Small Business Lending Fund," February 2, 2010, http://www.whitehouse.gov/the-press-office/president-obama-outlines-new-small-business-lending-fund.

[35] The White House, "Remarks by the President on the Monthly Job Numbers," May 7, 2010, http://m.whitehouse.gov/ the-press-office/remarks-president-monthly-jobs-numbers.

[36] H.R. 5297, the Small Business Jobs and Credit Act of 2010, Sec. 101. Small Business Lending Fund Purpose. In 2011, there were 7,513 FDIC-insured lending institutions in the United States. Of that number, 6,846 lending institutions had assets amounting to less than $1 billion (totaling $1.42 trillion), 561 lending institutions had assets of $1 billion to $10 billion (totaling $1.43 trillion), and 106 lending institutions had assets greater than $10 billion (totaling $10.76 trillion). See FDIC, "Quarterly Banking Profile: Second Quarter 2011," Washington, DC, http://www2.fdic.gov/qbp/2011jun/qbp.pdf.

[37] FDIC, "Quarterly Banking Profile: Fourth Quarter 2009," Washington, DC, http://www2. fdic.gov/qbp/2009dec/ qbp.pdf.

[38] Ibid. In the fourth quarter of 2009, 107 FDIC-insured lending institutions had assets greater than $10 billion.

[39] For further analysis of risk-weighted assets, see CRS Report R40249, Who Regulates Whom? An Overview of U.S. Financial Supervision, by Mark Jickling and Edward V. Murphy.

[40] If the appropriate banking agency would not otherwise recommend that the eligible institution receive the capital investment, the Secretary of the Treasury was authorized, in consultation with the appropriate banking agency, to consider allowing the eligible institution to participate in the program if the eligible institution provided matching capital from private, non-governmental sources that is equal to or greater than 100% of the SBLF investment and that matching capital was subordinate to the capital investment from the SBLF.

[41] H.R. 5297, the Small Business Lending Fund Act of 2010, Sec. 111. Assurances.

[42] H.R. 5297, the Small Business Lending Fund Act of 2010, Sec. 103. Small Business Lending Fund. Using a cost-based estimate, the Congressional Budget Office estimated that the SBLF would result in net outlays of $3.3 billion over 2010-1015, and would reduce outlays by $1.1 billion over the 2010-2020 period. Using an alternative fair-value estimate, the Congressional Budget Office estimated that the SBLF would result in net outlays of $6.2 billion over the 2010-2020 period. See U.S. Congressional Budget Office, "Cost Estimate: H.R. 5297, Small Business Lending Fund Act of 2010," Washington, DC, June 28, 2010, pp. 3, 4, http://www.cbo.gov/ftpdocs/115xx/doc11595/ hr5297_HousePassed.pdf.

[43] H.R. 5297, the Small Business Lending Fund Act of 2010, Sec. 102. Definitions.

[44] P.L. 111-240, the Small Business Jobs Act of 2010, Sec. 4102. Definitions.

[45] H.R. 5297, the Small Business Lending Fund Act of 2010, Sec. 102. Definitions.

[46] P.L. 111-240, the Small Business Jobs Act of 2010, Sec. 4102. Definitions.

[47] H.R. 5297, the Small Business Lending Fund Act of 2010, Sec. 103. Small Business Lending Fund.

[48] Ibid.
[49] Ibid.
[50] Ibid.
[51] P.L. 111-240, the Small Business Jobs Act of 2010, Sec. 4103. Small Business Lending Fund.
[52] H.R. 5297, the Small Business Lending Fund Act of 2010, Sec. 103. Small Business Lending Fund.
[53] P.L. 111-240, the Small Business Jobs Act of 2010, Sec. 4103. Small Business Lending Fund.
[54] H.R. 5297, the Small Business Lending Fund Act of 2010, Sec. 113. Temporary Amortization Authority.
[55] For additional information and analysis concerning P.L. 111-240, the Small Business Jobs Act of 2010, see CRS Report R40985, Small Business: Access to Capital and Job Creation, by Robert Jay Dilger.
[56] For further information and analysis concerning lender liquidity issues see CRS Report R41073, Government Interventions in Response to Financial Turmoil, by Baird Webel and Marc Labonte.
[57] H.Rept. 111-499, To Create the Small Business Lending Fund Program to Direct the Secretary of the Treasury to Make Capital Investments in Eligible Institutions in order to Increase the Availability of Credit for Small Businesses, and for other purposes, p. 16.
[58] Ibid., p. 37.
[59] Ibid., pp. 37, 38.
[60] Ibid., p. 38.
[61] Ibid.
[62] Representative Melissa Bean, "Consideration of the Small Business Jobs and Credit Act of 2010," House debate, Congressional Record, daily edition, vol. 156, no. 90 (June 16, 2010), p. H4514.
[63] Representative Nydia Velázquez, "Consideration of the Small Business Jobs and Credit Act of 2010," House debate, Congressional Record, daily edition, vol. 156, no. 90 (June 16, 2010), p. H4518.
[64] Ibid.
[65] Representative Randy Neugebauer, "Consideration of the Small Business Jobs and Credit Act of 2010," House debate, Congressional Record, daily edition, vol. 156, no. 90 (June 16, 2010), p. H4515.
[66] Senator Mary Landrieu, "Small Business Lending," remarks in the Senate, Congressional Record, daily edition, vol. 156, no. 108 (July 21, 2010), p. S6070.
[67] Ibid., p. S6071.
[68] Senator Olympia Snowe, "Small Business Lending," remarks in the Senate, Congressional Record, daily edition, vol. 156, no. 108 (July 22, 2010), pp. S6158.
[69] Ibid.
[70] Ibid., p. S6156.
[71] Senator Olympia Snowe, "Small Business Lending Fund Act of 2010," remarks in the Senate, Congressional Record, daily edition, vol. 156, no. 125 (September 16, 2010), pp. S7157.
[72] The act specified that the SBLF could not be used to provide loans greater than $10 million or that go to a business with more than $50 million in revenues. See P.L. 111-240, the Small Business Jobs Act of 2010, Sec. 4102. Definitions.
[73] Representative Sam Graves, "Full Committee Hearing, The State of Small Business Access to Credit and Capital: The View from Secretary Geithner," Letter to Members of the House Small Business Committee, Washington, DC, June 20, 2011, p. 19, http://smbiz.house.gov/UploadedFiles/6-22_Memo.pdf.

[74] Senator Kay Hagen, "Motion to Invoke Cloture on H.R. 5297, the Small Business Lending Fund Act of 2010," Rollcall Vote No. 236 Leg., Congressional Record, daily edition, vol. 156, part 125 (September 16, 2010), p. S7158; and Senator Al Franken, "Small Business Lending Fund Act of 2010," Rollcall Vote No. 237 Leg., Congressional Record, daily edition, vol. 156, part 125 (September 16, 2010), p. S7158.

[75] U.S. Office of Management and Budget, Budget of the United States Government, Fiscal Year 2012, Appendix: Department of the Treasury (Washington DC, GPO, 2011), p. 989, http:// www.whitehouse.gov/sites/default/files/omb/ budget/fy2012/assets/tre.pdf

[76] The Department of the Treasury based its forecast on an "analysis of demand for the program." See U.S. Department of the Treasury, "FY2012 Congressional Justification, Small Business Lending Fund," Washington, DC, page 7, http://www.treasury.gov/about/budget-performance/Documents/CJ_FY2012_SBLF_508.pdf

[77] Representative Sam Graves, Press Release, "Graves Questions Treasury Secretary Timothy Geithner on Access to Capital for Small Businesses," Washington, DC, June 22, 2011, http://www.smallbusiness.house.gov/News/ DocumentSingle.aspx?DocumentID=248058; and U.S. Congress, House Committee on Small Business, The State of Small Business Access to Capital and Credit: The View From Secretary Geithner, 112th Cong., 1st sess., June 22, 2011, Small Business Committee Document No. 112-023 (Washington: GPO, 2011), pp. 3, 9-11, 22, 25. Also see U.S. Government Accountability Office, Additional Actions Needed to Improve Transparency and Accountability, GAO-12- 183, December 14, 2011, http://www.gao.gov/products/GAO-12-183.

[78] Treasury and the federal banking agencies ultimately agreed that the banking agencies "would advise Treasury only on the financial viability of applicants and their capacity to increase small business lending, and that they would not make investment recommendations as they had for TARP. It was agreed that an applicant would be considered "viable" if it was (1) adequately capitalized; (2) not expected to become undercapitalized; and (3) not expected to be placed into conservatorship or receivership. Further, the [agencies'] validation of viability of an applicant would reflect only currently available supervisory information and rating assessments at the time the validation was made and would not predict Treasury's loss from making an investment in the institution." See U.S. Department of the Treasury, Office of the Inspector General. Small Business Lending Fund: Investment Decision Process for the Small Business Lending Fund, Washington, DC, May 13, 2011, p. 8, http://www.treasury.gov/about/organizational-structure/ig/Documents/ SBLF%20Report%20(OIG-SBLF-11-001).pdf.

[79] Internal Revenue Service, "Corporations," Washington, DC, http://www.irs.gov/ businesses/ small/article/0,,id= 98240,00.html.

[80] U.S. Department of the Treasury, Office of the Inspector General. Small Business Lending Fund: Investment Decision Process for the Small Business Lending Fund, Washington, DC, May 13, 2011, p. 7, http://www.treasury.gov/ about/organizational-structure/ig/Documents/ SBLF%20Report%20(OIG-SBLF-11-001).pdf..

[81] Internal Revenue Service, "S Corporations," Washington, DC, http://www.irs.gov/ businesses /small/article/0,,id= 98263,00.html.

[82] 12 C.F.R. §325.2: "Tier 1 capital or core capital means the sum of common stockholders' equity, noncumulative perpetual preferred stock (including any related surplus), and minority interests in consolidated subsidiaries, minus all intangible assets (other than mortgage servicing assets, nonmortgage servicing assets, and purchased credit card relationships eligible for inclusion in core capital pursuant to §325.5(f)), minus credit-enhancing interest-only strips that are not eligible for inclusion in core capital minus

deferred tax assets in excess of the limit set forth in §325.5(g), minus identified losses (to the extent that Tier 1 capital would have been reduced if the appropriate accounting entries to reflect the identified losses had been recorded on the insured depository institution's books), and minus investments in financial subsidiaries subject to 12 CFR part 362, subpart E, and minus the amount of the total adjusted carrying value of nonfinancial equity investments that is subject to a deduction from Tier 1 capital as set forth in section II.B.(6) of appendix A to this part."

[83] For further information and analysis of federal banking regulations see CRS Report R40249, Who Regulates Whom? An Overview of U.S. Financial Supervision, by Mark Jickling and Edward V. Murphy.

[84] U.S. Department of the Treasury, Office of the Inspector General. Small Business Lending Fund: Investment Decision Process for the Small Business Lending Fund, Washington, DC, May 13, 2011, p. 7, http://www.treasury.gov/ about/organizational-structure/ig/Documents/ SBLF%20Report%20(OIG-SBLF-11-001).pdf.

[85] Ibid.

[86] 12 C.F.R. Appendix A to Part 3 - Risk-Based Capital Guidelines: "The following elements comprise a national bank's Tier 2 capital: (1) Allowance for loan and lease losses, up to a maximum of 1.25% of risk-weighted assets, 3 subject to the transition rules in section 4(a)(2) of this appendix A; 3 The amount of the allowance for loan and lease losses that may be included in capital is based on a percentage of risk-weighted assets."

[87] U.S. Department of the Treasury, "Small Business Lending Fund Cost Report, Report to Congress submitted pursuant to Section 4106(2) of the Small Business Jobs Act of 2010," Washington, DC, July 19, 2011, p. 1, http://www.treasury.gov/resource-center/sb-programs/ DocumentsSBLFTransactions/ SBLF%204106(2)%20Cost%20Report.pdf.

[88] U.S. Department of the Treasury, "SBLF Investments as of September 27, 2011," Washington DC, http://www.treasury.gov/resource-center/sb-programs/DocumentsSBLFT ransactions/ SBLF_BiWeekly_Transactions_Report_THRU_09272011.pdf.

[89] Ibid.

[90] Ibid.

[91] P.L. 111-240, the Small Business Jobs Act of 2010, Sec. 4106. Reports.

[92] U.S. Department of the Treasury, "SBLF: Getting Started Guide," Washington DC, June 27, 2011, p. 13, http://www.treasury.gov/resource-center/sb-programs/Documents/SBLF%20 Getting%20Started%20Guide.pdf.

[93] Ibid.

[94] Ibid., p. 15.

[95] U.S. Department of the Treasury, "SBLF Quarterly 4106(3) Report – 4Q 2011," Washington, DC, http://www.treasury.gov/resource-center/sb-programs/DocumentsSBLFTransactions/ Use%20of%20Funds%204016(3)%20Report%20-%2001-09-12.pdf. SBLF institutions are also required to complete a short annual lending survey and provide annual certifications to Treasury that attest the accuracy of their reports, among other things.

[96] Ibid.

[97] U.S. Department of the Treasury, "SBLF: Getting Started Guide," Washington DC, June 27, 2011, p. 13, http://www.treasury.gov/resource-center/sb-programs/Documents/SBLF%20 Getting%20Started%20Guide.pdf.

[98] U.S. Department of the Treasury, "SBLF Quarterly 4106(3) Report – 4Q 2011," Washington, DC, pp. 1-3, http://www.treasury.gov/resource-center/sb-programs/DocumentsSBLFT ransactions/ Use%20of%20Funds%204016(3)%20Report%20-%2001-09-12.pdf.

[99] U.S. Department of the Treasury, "Small Business Lending Successes," Washington, DC, January 10, 2012, http://www.treasury.gov/connect/blog/Pages/Small-Business-Lending-Successes.aspx.

[100] Ibid.

[101] Harry Terris, "Former TARP Banks Lag Peers in SBLF Lending," American Banker, Vol. 177, No. 16, January 25, 2012.

[102] Kate Davidson, "Was the SBLF Program a Success?" American Banker, Vol. 177, No. 8, January 12, 2012.

[103] U.S. Senator Olympia Snowe, "Snowe Calls for Comprehensive Fixes to Small Business Lending Fund," Washington DC, March 30, 2011, http://snowe.senate.gov /public/ index.cfm/pressreleases?ContentRecord_id= b1507369-8193-44ff-94ae-ceb94d5debe8& ContentType_id=ae7a6475-a01f-4da5-aa94-0a98973de620&Group_id= 2643ccf9-0d03-4d09-9082-3807031cb84a&MonthDisplay=3&YearDisplay=2011.

[104] Current law provides the Treasury Secretary the discretion to extend the repayment period beyond 10 years. P.L. 111-240, the Small Business Jobs Act of 2010, Sec. 4103(d)(5)(h); 12 U.S.C. § 4741.

[105] Current law does not include a termination date for the program, other than terminating the authority to make capital investments in eligible institutions one year after the date of enactment. P.L. 111-240, the Small Business Jobs Act of 2010, Sec. 4109. Termination and Continuation of Authorities.

[106] Current law requires the Treasury Secretary to consult with appropriate financial regulators to determine if the eligible institution may receive a capital investment under the program. P.L. 111-240, the Small Business Jobs Act of 2010, Sec. 4103(d); 12 U.S.C. § 4741.

[107] Senator Snowe indicated that this change "would address concerns that the existing benchmark may be too low, by historical standards, and that an adjustment could result in additional small business lending. See U.S. Senator Olympia Snowe, "Snowe Calls for Comprehensive Fixes to Small Business Lending Fund," Washington DC, March 30, 2011, http://snowe.senate.gov/public/index.cfm/pressreleases?ContentRecord_id=b1507369-8193-44ff-94ae-ceb94d5debe8& ContentType_id=ae7a6475-a01f-4da5-aa94-0a98973de620&Group_id=2643ccf9-0d03-4d09-9082-3807031cb84a& MonthDisplay=3&YearDisplay=2011.

[108] H.R. 2807, the Small Business Leg-Up Act of 2011.

[109] U.S. Department of the Treasury, Office of the Inspector General. Small Business Lending Fund: Investment Decision Process for the Small Business Lending Fund, Washington, DC, May 13, 2011, http://www.treasury.gov/ about/organizational-structure/ig/Documents/ SBLF%20Report%20(OIG-SBLF-11-001).pdf; and U.S. Department of the Treasury, Office of the Inspector General. Small Business Lending Fund: Treasury Should Consider Concerns Regarding Participants Management and Historical Retained Earnings When Estimating the Cost of the SBLF Program, Washington, DC, December 22, 2011, http://www.treasury.gov/about/organizational-structure/ig/ Agency%20Documents/Cost%20of%20SBLF%20Program%20-%20Final%20Report% 20for%20Internet.pdf.

[110] P.L. 111-240, the Small Business Jobs Act of 2010, Sec. 4107. Oversight and Audits.

[111] Representative Sam Graves, "Full Committee Hearing, The State of Small Business Access to Credit and Capital: The View from Secretary Geithner," Letter to Members of the House Small Business Committee, Washington, DC, June 20, 2011, p. 19, http://smbiz.house.gov/UploadedFiles/6-22_Memo.pdf.

[112] Program administrative costs (e.g., monitoring the performance and compliance of participants, reporting on the program's performance and costs, and managing the securities purchased through the SBLF program) must be excluded from subsidy cost estimates in accordance with guidelines in the Federal Credit Reform Act of 1990. See OMB Circular A-11, section 185.2.

[113] U.S. Department of the Treasury, Office of the Inspector General. Small Business Lending Fund: Treasury Should Consider Concerns Regarding Participants Management and Historical Retained Earnings When Estimating the Cost of the SBLF Program, Washington, DC, December 22, 2011, pp. 1-3, http://www.treasury.gov/about/organizationalstructure/ig/ Agency%20Documents/Cost%20of%20SBLF%20Program%20-%20Final%20Report%20for%20Internet.pdf.

[114] U.S. Department of the Treasury, Office of the Inspector General. Small Business Lending Fund: Investment Decision Process for the Small Business Lending Fund, Washington, DC, May 13, 2011, p. 19, http://www.treasury.gov/about/organizational-structure/ig/ Documents /SBLF%20Report%20(OIG-SBLF-11-001).pdf.

[115] Ibid., pp. 19, 20.

[116] Ibid., p. 20.

[117] Ibid., p. 25.

In: The Small Business Lending Fund ISBN 978-1-62257-212-0
Editors: J. A. Bell and C. M. Richardson ©2012 Nova Science Publishers, Inc.

Chapter 2

SMALL BUSINESS LENDING FUND: USE OF FUNDS REPORTS*

The Department of the Treasury

OVERVIEW

Small businesses are a vital part of the American economy and their success is a critical component of the economic recovery. Established by the Small Business Jobs Act of 2010 (the Act), the Small Business Lending Fund (SBLF) is a dedicated fund designed to provide capital to qualified community banks[1] and community development loan funds (CDLFs) in order to encourage small business lending. The purpose of the SBLF is to encourage Main Street banks and small businesses to work together, help create jobs, and promote economic growth in communities across the nation.

This report provides information on changes in small business lending by SBLF participants as of December 31, 2011, relative to baseline levels.[2] Additionally, this report provides information on changes in business lending and other lending by SBLF banks, including a comparison of increases in business lending by these banks, a group of non-SBLF banks, and the subset of SBLF banks that refinanced into the program from Treasury's Capital Purchase Program (CPP).

* This is an edited, reformatted and augmented version of Use of Funds Report, Report to Congress submitted pursuant to Section 4106(3) of the Small Business Jobs Act, dated April 2012.

As of December 31, 2011, institutions participating in SBLF have made important progress in increasing their small business lending, helping to support small businesses and local economies across the nation.

- In total, SBLF participants have increased their small business lending by $4.8 billion over a $36.0 billion baseline, and by $1.3 billion over the prior quarter.
- Increases in small business lending are widespread across SBLF participants, with 84 percent of participants having increased their small business lending over baseline levels.
- A substantial majority of SBLF participants — more than 68 percent — have increased their small business lending by 10 percent or more.

As of December 31, 2011, the 281 banks participating in SBLF have increased their business lending more than a comparison group of non-SBLF banks.

- SBLF banks have increased business loans outstanding by a median of 21.5 percent over baseline levels, versus a 1.1 percent median increase for the group of non-SBLF banks.
- SBLF banks have increased business lending by substantially greater amounts than the comparison group of non-SBLF banks across median measures of size, geography, and loan type.
- SBLF banks that refinanced CPP funding have increased business lending by a median of 20.2 percent since their initial receipt of CPP funding from Treasury. Over that period, these participants have increased their business lending by $5.8 billion.

Background and Methodology

This report is submitted to Congress pursuant to Section 4106(3) of the Act, which directs the Secretary of the Treasury to provide a quarterly written report on how institutions participating in the SBLF program have used the funds they received under the program.

Treasury invested over $4.0 billion in 332 institutions through the SBLF program. These amounts include investments of $3.9 billion in 281 community banks and $104 million in 51 CDLFs. Collectively, these institutions operate in over 3,000 locations across 48 states.

The initial disbursement of SBLF funding to banks occurred on June 21, 2011, with subsequent transactions completed thereafter until the program's September 27, 2011 statutory funding deadline.

The SBLF program encourages lending to small businesses by providing capital to community banks and CDLFs with less than $10 billion in assets.

- For community banks, the SBLF is structured to encourage small business lending through a dividend or interest rate incentive structure. The initial rate payable on SBLF capital is, at most, 5 percent, and the rate falls to 1 percent if a bank's small business lending increases by 10 percent or more. [3] Banks that increase their lending by less than 10 percent pay rates between 2 percent and 4 percent. If a bank's lending does not increase in the first two years, however, the rate increases to 7 percent. If a bank has not repaid the SBLF funding after four and a half years, the rate increases to 9 percent.
- For CDLFs, the SBLF is structured to encourage small business lending through access to low-cost capital at a 2 percent interest rate. These non-profit loan funds play a critical role in distressed communities across the country that lack access to mainstream financial services. CDLFs engage in activities ranging from offering microloans to entrepreneurs, providing mezzanine debt to growing small businesses, and financing community facilities like charter schools and health clinics.

Definition of Small Business Lending

The Act defines "small business lending" as business loans that are (a) $10 million or less in amount to businesses with $50 million or less in revenue and (b) included in one of the following categories: (i) commercial and industrial loans, (ii) owner-occupied nonfarm, nonresidential real estate loans, (iii) loansto finance agricultural production and other loans to farmers, and (iv) loans secured by farmland.

The SBLF program terms provide for additional adjustments to the calculation of small business lending relating to net charge-offs and portions of loans guaranteed by the US government or for which risk has been assumed by third parties, as well as mergers and acquisitions and purchases of loans.

Changes in Small Business Lending

In this report, changes in small business lending are calculated as the difference between the level of loans outstanding as of December 31, 2011, and the baseline amount. Participants report changes in small business lending by submitting quarterly supplemental reports to Treasury. The most recent supplemental report includes lending information as of December 31, 2011.

Definition of Business Lending

In contrast to small business lending, "business lending" refers to the same four categories of loans referenced in the definition of small business lending without exclusions for loans to businesses over $10 million and loans to businesses with $50 million in revenue, and without the additional adjustments used in SBLF's calculation of small business lending.

Changes in Business Lending

This report describes changes in "business lending" by bank participants and by a comparison group of non-SBLF banks relative to baseline levels.[4] Except where noted, the baseline measurement for changes in business lending is calculated as the average of the amounts that were reported for each of the four calendar quarters ended June 30, 2010. Changes in business lending are calculated as the difference between the level of loans outstanding as of December 31, 2011, and the baseline amount.

Because non-SBLF participants do not report small business lending as defined by the Act, this report compares business lending as defined herein. Most "business lending" reported by SBLF bank participants qualifies as "small business lending." As of December 31, 2011, small business lending (as defined by the program terms) totaled 95.0 percent of business lending for the median SBLF bank.

Non-SBLF Bank Comparison Group

In describing changes in business lending, this report compares the group of 281 banks that received SBLF funding to a comparison group across median measures of loan growth.

The comparison group is comprised of the 6,522 non-SBLF insured depository institutions that were established prior to September 30, 2009, had total assets between $7.0 million and $6.4 billion (the range of total assets for SBLF banks) as of Mar h 31, 2011 (which is the end of the first quarter prior to SBLF banks receiving funding), and are located in one of the jurisdictions (44 states and the District of Columbia) in which SBLF banks are headquartered.

While the comparison group includes banks that share the aforementioned characteristics with SBLF banks, the selection criteria for the group does not imply that it matches the size or geographic distribution of SBLF banks. The comparison group may have different financial and supervisory characteristics, among other factors.

INCREASES IN SMALL BUSINESS LENDING OVER BASELINE LEVELS

As of December 31, 2011, SBLF participants have increased their small business lending by $4.8 billion over their aggregate baseline. Bank participants have increased their small business lending by $4.7 billion (or 13.4 percent) over a $35.2 billion baseline, and CDLFs increased their small business lending by $95.4 million (or 12.1 percent) over a $786.8 million baseline.

The following table shows the aggregate increase in qualified small business lending reported by SBLF participants as of December 31, 2011.

Increases in small business lending are widespread among SBLF participants.

To date, 235 of the 281 participating community banks (or 84 percent) and 43 of the 51 CDLFs (or 84 percent) have increased their small business lending. In addition, a substantial majority of SBLF participants — more than 68 percent of participants — have now increased their small business lending by 10 percent or more.

Twenty-four additional institutions have now increased lending by more than 10 percent in the fourth quarter of 2011.

Increase in Small Business Lending over Baseline by SBLF Participants
(Reported as of 4Q 2011)

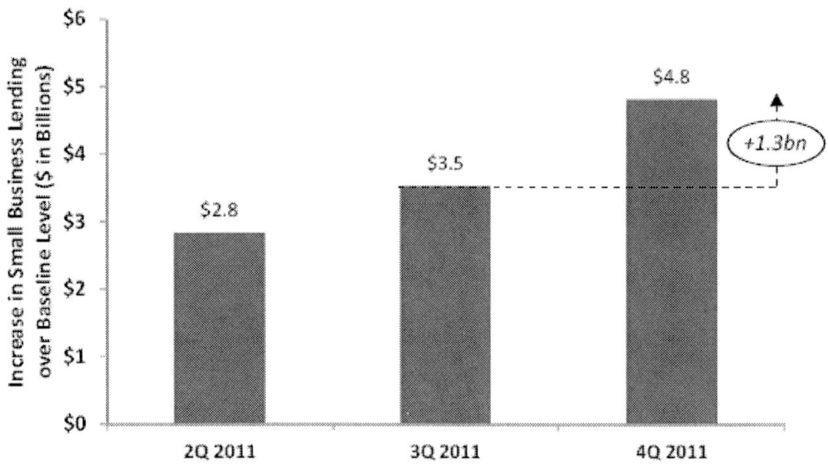

SBLF Participants Reporting Increases in Small Business Lending over Baseline
(Reported as of 3Q 2011 and 4Q 2011)

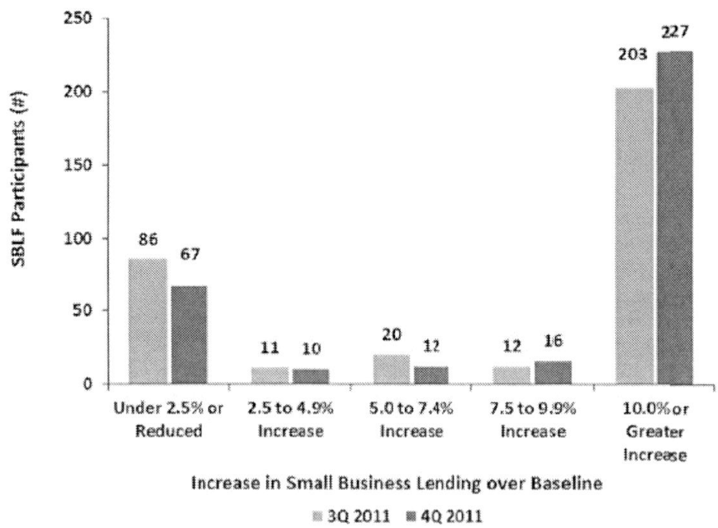

The chart on the following page shows quarter-over-quarter changes in the number of participants reporting lending in the five ranges of small business loan growth that correspond to various dividend or interest rates payable on SBLF securities. Institution-specific reporting of small business lending by banks and CDLFs participating in SBLF is attached to this report.

COMPARISON OF LENDING BY SBLF BANKS AND NON-SBLF BANKS[5]

SBLF banks have increased business lending by greater amounts than the comparison group of non-SBLF banks across median measures of size, geography, and loan type.

SBLF banks also report a median increase in other (non-business related) types of lending, while the comparison group of non-SBLF banks shows a median decrease in such lending.

Overall Increases in Business Lending and Other Lending

Comparing the level of loans outstanding as of December 31, 2011 to their baseline levels, SBLF banks increased business lending by a median of 21.5 percent, versus a 1.1 percent median increase for the comparison group of non-SBLF banks. In addition to increasing business lending, SBLF banks increased other types of lending by a median of 9.5 percent over baseline levels, versus a median decrease of 3.9 percent among the group of non-SBLF banks.

The following graph shows increases in business lending and other lending by SBLF banks and the comparison group of non-SBLF banks.

Distribution of Increases in Business Lending

A substantially greater percentage of SBLF banks than the comparison group of non-SBLF banks report significant increases in business lending. In total, 69.4 percent of banks participating in SBLF have increased their business lending by 10 percent or more versus 33.5 percent for the comparison group of non-SBLF banks.

47.7 percent of the non-SBLF banks have reduced business lending versus 16.8 percent of the SBLF banks.

Increases in Business Lending and Other Lending
(Reported as of 4Q 2011)

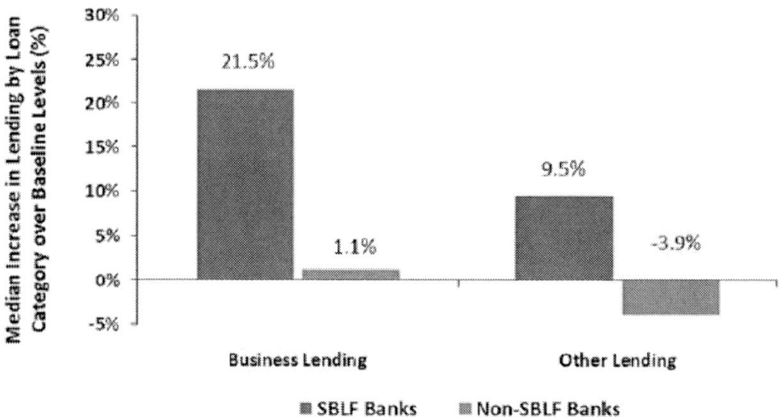

Distribution of Changes in Business Lending
(Reported as of 4Q 2011)

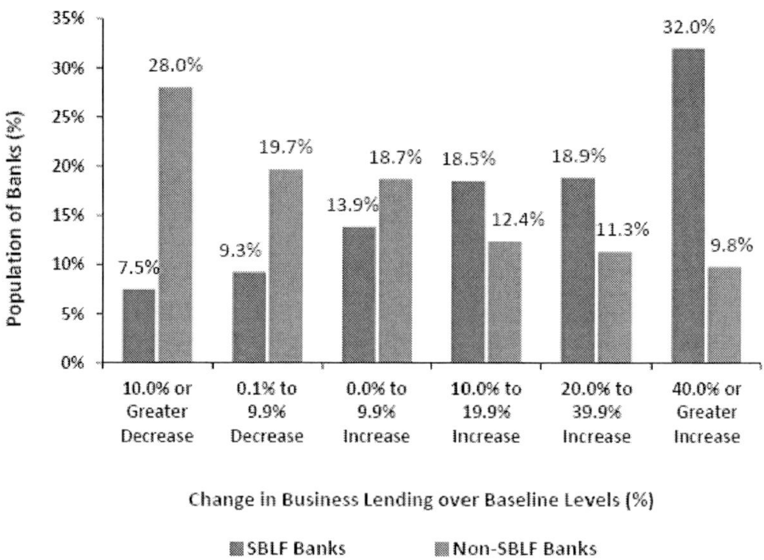

SBLF banks increased business lending to a greater extent than non-SBLF banks, measured by the proportion of institutions reporting increases, as well as the percentage increases reported. SBLF banks increased business lending by a mean of 41.7 percent with a standard deviation of 130.3.[6] The comparison group of non-SBLF banks increased business lending by a mean of 14.8 percent with a standard deviation of 195.7.

Increases in Business Lending by Regional Geography

In each region[7] of the country, SBLF banks reported greater median increases in business lending than the comparison group of non-SBLF banks.

The following graph compares median increases in business lending by SBLF banks with the comparison group of non-SBLF banks across four regions.

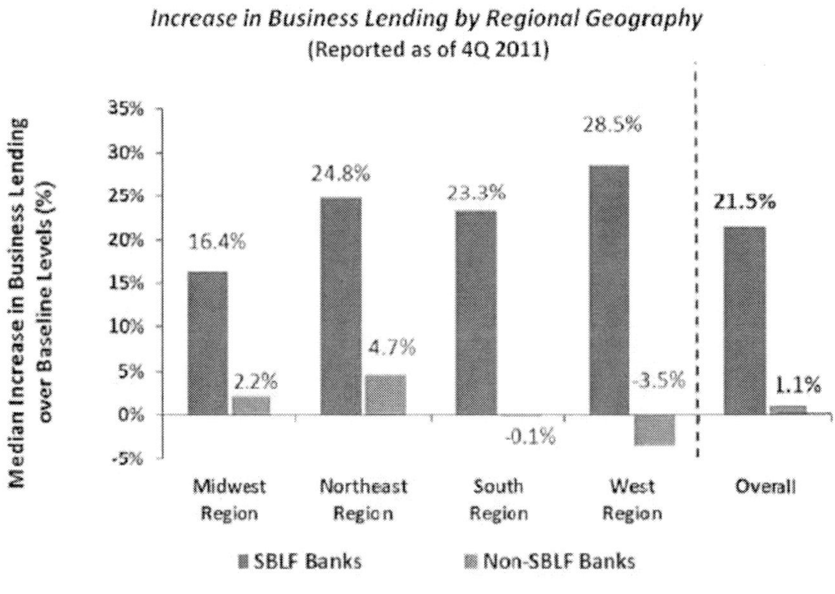

Increases in Business Lending by Institution Size

Across all ranges of institution size as defined by total assets, SBLF banks reported greater median increases in business lending than the comparison group of non-SBLF banks.

The following graph compares median increases in business lending by SBLF banks and the comparison group of non-SBLF banks across four categories of institution size.

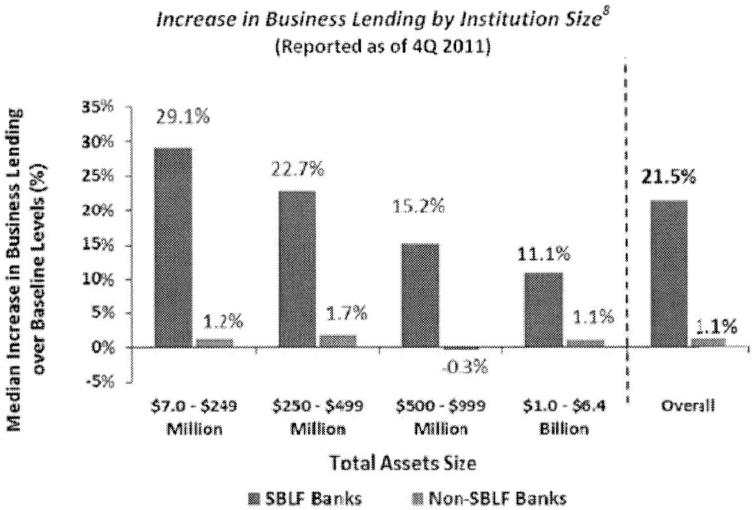

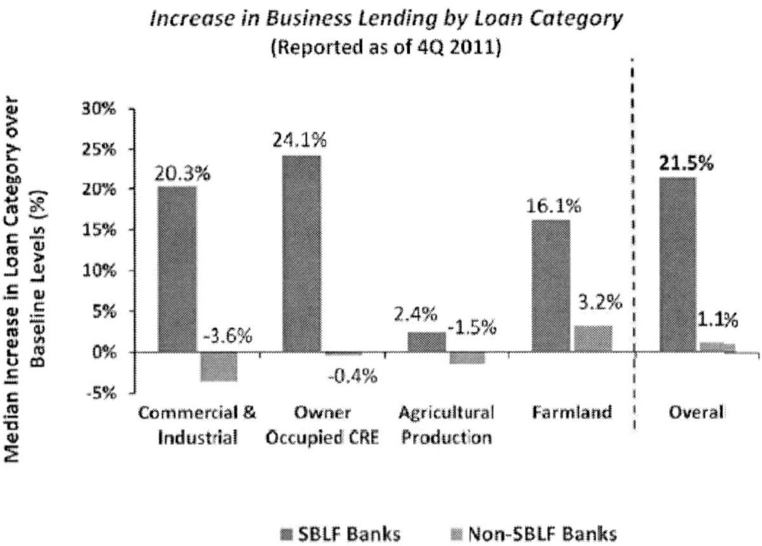

Increases in Business Lending by Loan Category

Across each of the four loan categories that comprise business lending, SBLF banks reported greater median increases in business lending than the comparison group of non-SBLF banks.

The following graph compares median increases in business lending by SBLF banks and the comparison group of non-SBLF banks across the four categories of business loans.

Lending by Former Capital Purchase Program (CPP) Participants

The Act authorized Treasury to allow CPP participants that met certain requirements to refinance CPP investments into SBLF. In total, 137 institutions repaid a CPP investment in connection with an SBLF closing. These banks received $2.7 billion in SBLF funding and used $2.2 billion of this capital to repay outstanding CPP balances.

Lending Increases by Institutions that Refinanced CPP Investments

Banks that received CPP funding and refinanced these investments through SBLF reported a significant median increase in business lending following receipt of the initial CPP investments. These institutions also reported a median increase from the SBLF baseline period.

SBLF banks that refinanced CPP funding reported a median increase in business lending of 20.2 percent since their initial receipt of CPP funding from Treasury. These participants also reported that their business lending has increased by a median of 12.5 percent since the baseline period. The comparison group of non-SBLF banks reported a median increase in business lending of 5.5 percent since the reporting date following the CPP closings. Since the baseline period, the comparison group has increased business lending by a median of 1.1 percent, as previously noted.

Dividend Rates Payable by Institutions that Refinanced CPP Investments

Institutions that refinance capital from CPP benefit from the dividend rate incentive provided in SBLF only if they increase their small business lending over baseline levels. As of December 31, 2011, banks that refinanced CPP capital pay an average dividend (or interest rate) of 2.9 percent on SBLF funding, whereas other bank participants pay an average rate of 2.0 percent.[10]

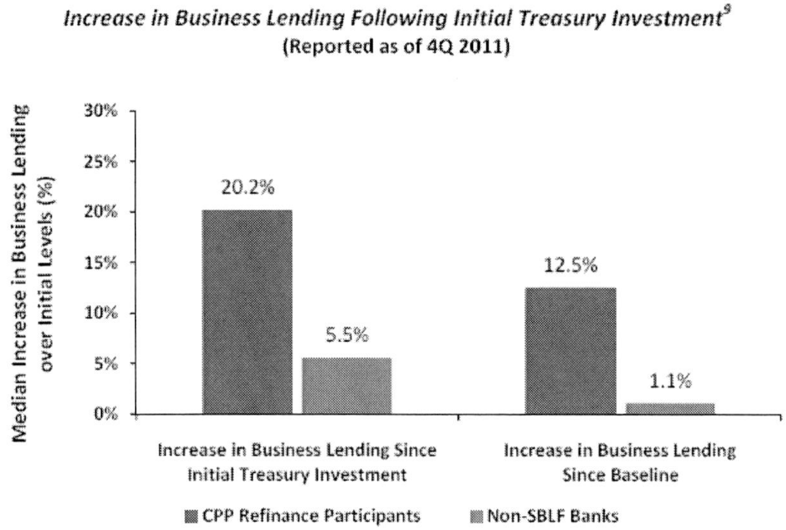

End Notes

[1] In this report, the terms "banks" and "community banks" encompass banks, thrifts, and bank and thrift holding companies with consolidated assets of less than $10 billion.

[2] In this report, the terms "small business lending" and "business lending" are defined in the "Background & Methodology" section of this report. As established in the Act, the baseline for measuring the change in small business lending is the average of the amounts that were reported for each of the four calendar quarters ended June 30, 2010. Participants report changes in small business lending by submitting quarterly supplemental reports to Treasury. The most recent supplemental reports include lending information as of December 31, 2011.

[3] The initial interest rate paid by S corporations and mutual institutions is, at most, 7.7 percent. If these institutions increase their small business lending by 10 percent or more, then the rate falls to as low as 1.5 percent. These interest rates equate to after-tax effective rates (assuming a 35% tax rate) equivalent to the dividend rate paid by C corporation participants.

[4] Insured depository institutions are required each quarter to file a Consolidated Report of Condition and Income or Thrift Financial Report (collectively, "call reports"), as applicable. Among other financial information, quarterly call reports include data on the lending of an insured depository institution. Information in this report regarding business lending was retrieved from call reports filed for the quarter ending December 31, 2011.

[5] This comparative information is provided in addition to the program's statutorily required historical reporting on changes in participants' small business lending and will be updated periodically.

[6] The standard deviation is a measure of the variation of data points from their mean. In these results, the large standard deviations indicate that the percentage increases in business lending by SBLF banks and the comparison group of non-SBLF banks are distributed over a large range of values and not concentrated around the mean.

[7] In this report, the Midwest Region includes: Illinois, Indiana, Iowa, Kansas, Michigan, Minnesota, Missouri, Nebraska, North Dakota, Ohio, South Dakota, and Wisconsin. The Northeast Region includes: Connecticut, Maine, Massachusetts, New Hampshire, New Jersey, New York, and Pennsylvania. The South Region includes: Alabama, Arkansas, Delaware, District of Columbia, Florida, Georgia, Kentucky, Louisiana, Maryland, Mississippi, North Carolina, Oklahoma, South Carolina, Tennessee, Texas, Virginia, and West Virginia. The West Region includes: Arizona, California, Colorado, Idaho, Montana, Nevada, Utah, Washington, and Wyoming.

[8] In this report, institution size (including the size ranges in this graph) are based on the total assets reported by banks as of March 31, 2011, the quarter immediately prior to Treasury's first SBLF investment.

[9] For the 137 CPP refinance participants, the median increase in business lending reflected in the first column is measured from the first reporting date after each participant received its initial CPP capital to December 31, 2011. Because the median CPP refinance participant received this capital during the first quarter of 2009, the median increase in business lending for the comparison group of 6,522 non-SBLF banks is measured from March 31, 2009 to December 31, 2011 for this calculation.

[10] These figures are adjusted to account for differences in the rates paid by subchapter S corporations and mutual institutions.

In: The Small Business Lending Fund ISBN 978-1-62257-212-0
Editors: J. A. Bell and C. M. Richardson

Chapter 3

SMALL BUSINESS LENDING FUND: ADDITIONAL ACTIONS NEEDED TO IMPROVE TRANSPARENCY AND ACCOUNTABILITY*

United States Government Accountability Office

WHY GAO DID THIS STUDY

The Small Business Jobs Act of 2010 aimed to stimulate job growth by establishing the Small Business Lending Fund program (SBLF) within the U.S. Department of the Treasury (Treasury), among other activities. The SBLF program was designed to encourage community banks and community development loan funds with assets of less than $10 billion to increase their lending to small businesses.

The act also requires GAO to audit SBLF annually. This initial report examines (1) Treasury's procedures for evaluating applications for SBLF funds, (2) characteristics of institutions that applied for and received funds from SBLF and factors that influenced banks' decision to participate, and (3) Treasury's plans to monitor participants and measure SBLF's progress in increasing small business lending. GAO reviewed documents on Treasury's

---

* This is an edited, reformatted and augmented version of the Highlights of GAO-12-183, a report to congressional committees, dated December 2011.

procedures and controls; analyzed data on applicants; compared SBLF banks with a peer group of nonparticipating banks; surveyed a representative sample of banks (for a weighted response rate of 66 percent); and interviewed Treasury, federal banking regulators, and representatives from industry associations.

What GAO Recommends

To improve transparency and accountability, Treasury should (1) enhance its strategy for communicating with participants and other stakeholders, (2) finalize procedures for monitoring participants' compliance with program requirements, and (3) complete plans for assessing the program's effectiveness. Treasury agreed with GAO's recommendations.

What GAO Found

Treasury adopted procedures to help ensure that applicants were evaluated consistently and were likely to repay funds, but its lack of clarity in explaining program requirements and decisions created confusion among applicants. The evaluation process included input from federal and state regulators, reviews of small business lending plans, and estimates of the applicants' ability to repay funds. GAO's analysis of the inputs Treasury relied on for its decisions showed that Treasury generally followed its process, although additional steps were taken for some applicants, such as revising repayment estimates to include updated information provided by federal regulators. Also, Treasury's initial announcement of program requirements did not make clear that applicants could not have restrictions on paying dividends, affecting over 200 applicants. Treasury also did not explain the rationale for its funding decisions to applicants and other stakeholders, and many applicants who were not approved were not notified until September 2011—almost 4 months after the application deadline and initial disbursements of funds. Although Treasury had several outreach efforts to communicate with the public about SBLF, such efforts have not always been timely or clear to applicants and other stakeholders and could contribute to SBLF being poorly understood by the public and Congress.

Fewer institutions applied to SBLF and received funding than initially anticipated, in part because many banks did not anticipate that demand for small business loans would increase. SBLF was authorized to invest up to $30 billion, but Treasury funded just 332 of the 935 applications, investing about $4 billion, or 13 percent, of the authorized funds. The institutions that applied to and were funded by SBLF were primarily institutions with total assets of less than $500 million. In addition, GAO's analysis showed that compared with banks that did not apply to SBLF, funded banks had fewer problem loans and small loans (under $1 million) and less capital. GAO's nationally representative survey of community banks showed that respondents' most common reason for not applying to the SBLF program was a lack of demand for small business loans.

Treasury has not finalized plans for assessing SBLF's impact on small business lending or procedures for monitoring recipients for compliance with program requirements. GAO's analysis shows that credit is still difficult to obtain, although it has eased some compared with 2009, confirming that the lending environment remains challenging. Such an environment makes Treasury's planned monitoring and assessments increasingly important. Treasury officials told GAO that they have been developing procedures for monitoring compliance, but they are not yet finalized. Similarly, Treasury is considering various options for evaluating SBLF's performance, but complex economic relationships will make linking the SBLF program to job growth difficult. Treasury officials said that they had been focused on approving applicants and disbursing funds by the statutory deadline of September 27, 2011, and that finalizing procedures and performance indicators had lagged as a result. Now that funding decisions and disbursements have been made, finalizing plans for monitoring compliance and assessing SBLF's progress can take precedence. Without a full and robust assessment, Treasury will not be able to provide useful information to policymakers about the participants' compliance and the effectiveness of a capital infusion program as a means of increasing small business lending.

ABBREVIATIONS

ABA	American Bankers Association
call reports	consolidated reports of condition and income

CAMELS	C-Capital adequacy, A-Asset quality, M-Management quality, E–Earnings, L–Liquidity, and S-Sensitivity to market risk
CDCI	community development capital initiative
CDFI	community development financial institution
CDLF	Community Development Loan Funds
CPP	Capital Purchase Program
FDIC	Federal Deposit Insurance Corporation
Federal Reserve	Board of Governors of the Federal Reserve System
GPRA	Government Performance and Results Act of 1993
ICBA	Independent Community Bankers Association
NFIB	National Federation of Independent Business
OCC	Office of the Comptroller of the Currency
OTS	Office of Thrift Supervision
SBLF	Small Business Lending Fund
SBLI	Small Business Lending Index
SNL	SNL Financial–collects and publishes financial data and analyses
TARP	Troubled Asset Relief Program
Treasury	Department of the Treasury
IG	Inspector General

December 14, 2011

Congressional Committees

Congressional interest in assisting small businesses has increased in recent years, primarily because of continued concerns about unemployment and the sustainability of the current economic recovery. In particular, Congress has grown increasingly concerned that in the current economic recovery small businesses might not be able to access enough capital to create needed jobs. In 2008 and early 2009, major disruptions of business credit markets made accessing credit difficult for small businesses. For example, a Wells Fargo survey shows that the number of small businesses having difficulty accessing credit more than tripled from 2007 to 2010, with ultimately almost 40 percent of small businesses indicating that credit was difficult to obtain. Further, the Secretary of the Treasury testified in June 2011 that small businesses were concentrated in sectors that had been especially hard hit by the recession, including construction-related industries. As a result, during the depths of the 2007-2009 crisis, the rate of job losses was almost twice as high for small businesses as it was for larger firms.[1]

To address these concerns, on September 27, 2010, President Obama signed into law the Small Business Jobs Act of 2010.[2] Among other things, this legislation aims to stimulate job growth by establishing the Small Business Lending Fund program (SBLF). The SBLF program is designed to encourage banks and community development loan funds (CDLF) with assets of less than $10 billion to increase their lending to small businesses with up to $50 million in annual revenues.[3] The act authorizes the Treasury Secretary to make up to $30 billion of capital available and offers incentives to increase small business lending.

Although the SBLF program has received support from some members of Congress and banking and business trade groups, other congressional members and groups have raised concerns about the program. These concerns include protecting taxpayer money (that is, ensuring that the funds will be paid back), ensuring that only healthy institutions have access to the funds, and ensuring that the institutions receiving the funds will actually increase new business lending. Some others have also expressed concerns that allowing institutions that received funds under the Troubled Asset Relief Program (TARP) to draw on SBLF funds would offer a way to refinance out of TARP with lower dividend rates and fewer program restrictions but without any guarantee of increasing business lending. Legislation has been introduced in Congress intended to address program concerns.[4]

The 2010 Small Business Jobs Act requires GAO to conduct an annual audit of the SBLF program. Under this statutory mandate, this initial report assesses (1) the Department of the Treasury's (Treasury) procedures to implement SBLF and evaluate applications for SBLF funds, (2) characteristics of institutions applying for and receiving SBLF funds and the factors that influenced banks' decision to participate, and (3) Treasury's plans to monitor SBLF participants and measure the SBLF's progress in increasing small business lending.

To assess Treasury's evaluation process for SBLF applications, we reviewed Treasury's policies, procedures, and internal controls for SBLF, including nonpublic documents and publicly available material from the SBLF website. We reviewed Treasury's and the four federal banking regulators'—Federal Deposit Insurance Corporation (FDIC), Board of Governors of the Federal Reserve System (Federal Reserve), the Office of the Comptroller of the Currency (OCC), and the Office of Thrift Supervision (OTS)—respective roles and responsibilities and compared them with their roles for the Capital

Purchase Program (CPP), a capital infusion program under TARP that is similar to SBLF.[5] To identify applicants that fell outside of Treasury's stated evaluation parameters, we analyzed data that Treasury used to inform its funding decisions, including CAMELS composite ratings, repayment probabilities, performance ratios, lending plan scores, dividend restriction information, and results of regulators' financial condition assessments.[6] We also analyzed data from Treasury, FDIC, and SNL Financial (SNL)—a financial institution database—for all applicants. We then compared the applicants that Treasury approved and did not approve to its evaluation thresholds and identified a number of approved and nonapproved applicants that fell outside of these general parameters. Using the results of this analysis, we then selected a judgmental sample of 15 applicants that appeared to be particularly out of line with the parameters Treasury had set for additional review. We obtained the relevant minutes from Treasury's Application Review Committee and Investment Committee for these 15 applicants to review Treasury's rationale for their decisions on these applicants. We interviewed Treasury officials for further clarification. We also interviewed representatives of industry trade groups to obtain their perspectives on SBLF and the application process. Our criteria for assessing Treasury's evaluation process drew from GAO's Standards for *Internal Control in the Federal Government* and past IG and GAO work, particularly on CPP.[7]

To describe the characteristics of the institutions that applied to and received SBLF program funds, we analyzed data from Treasury on applicants and participants, including the number of institutions that were approved, not approved, and those that were refinancing their CPP or CDCI funds through SBLF.[8] We also analyzed the geographic distribution of participants and assessed the extent to which institutions receiving SBLF funds tended to be located in high unemployment areas. We also developed a comparable peer group of banks that did not apply for SBLF program funds and compared their financial condition and past lending patterns with those of SBLF program applicants and participants that are also banks. The data we analyzed from Treasury, FDIC, and regulatory filings were sufficiently reliable to describe the characteristics of SBLF bank applicants and their peers. Finally, we conducted a Web-based survey of a nationally representative sample of banks with assets of $10 billion or less to obtain their reasons for applying or not applying to the program. The weighted response rate was 66 percent.[9] On the basis of our application of generally accepted survey design practices, we determined that the data collected via our survey were of sufficient quality for our purposes.

To assess Treasury's plans to measure SBLF's effectiveness, we interviewed Treasury officials about their intended work. To describe trends in small business lending, we used a number of indicators that provide a variety of perspectives on small business credit market conditions leading up to the implementation of SBLF. Appendix I contains more information on our objectives, scope, and methodology.

We conducted this performance audit from December 2010 to December 2011 in Washington, D.C., in accordance with generally accepted government auditing standards. Those standards require that we plan and perform the audit to obtain sufficient, appropriate evidence to provide a reasonable basis for our findings and conclusions based on our audit objectives. We believe that the evidence obtained provides a reasonable basis for our findings and conclusions based on our audit objectives.

BACKGROUND

SBLF Goals, Considerations, and Eligibility Requirements

SBLF was one of the key provisions under the 2010 Small Business Jobs Act to address the ongoing effects of the financial crisis on small businesses. The act provided temporary authority to the Secretary of the Treasury to make capital investments in eligible banks and CDLFs in order to increase the availability of credit for small businesses. The legislation directed Treasury to consider the following in exercising its authorities for the SBLF program:

- increasing the availability of credit for small businesses;
- providing funding to minority-owned eligible institutions and other eligible institutions that served small businesses that were minority-, veteran-, and women-owned and that also served low- and moderate-income, minority, and other underserved or rural communities;
- protecting and increasing American jobs;
- increasing the opportunity for small business development in high-unemployment areas;
- ensuring that all eligible institutions can apply, without regard to geographic location;
- providing transparency with respect to the use of SBLF funds;
- minimizing costs to taxpayers;

- promoting and engaging in financial education for would-be borrowers; and
- providing funding to eligible institutions that served small businesses directly affected by the Deepwater Horizon spill.

SBLF is intended to increase small business lending. For the purposes of the program, the legislation defined qualified small business lending—as defined in an institution's quarterly regulatory filings (call reports)—as one of the following:[10]

- commercial and industrial loans;
- owner-occupied nonfarm, nonresidential real estate loans;
- loans to finance agricultural production and other loans to farmers; and
- loans secured by farmland.

In addition, qualifying loans cannot be for more than $10 million, and the business may not have more than $50 million in revenue.[11]

The act specifically restricts applications from institutions that are on the FDIC problem bank list (i.e., defined in the act as banks with a composite CAMELS ratings of 4 or 5) or have been removed from that list in the previous 90 days.[12] Treasury determines whether to provide SBLF funding to a bank after consulting with the appropriate federal and, if applicable, state banking regulator. The Small Business Jobs Act outlined different statutory financial eligibility criteria for CDLFs. To qualify for SBLF, CDLFs must meet a number of requirements, including having at least 3 years of operating experience.

SBLF Application Process and Requirements

Applicants submitted a 1-page application to Treasury and a 3-page small business lending plan to their primary federal regulator to (1) describe how they would use SBLF funds to address the needs of small businesses in the communities they served; (2) specify the projected increase in small business lending they expected to achieve 2 years after receiving SBLF funds; and (3) describe their approach to community outreach and advertising for small business lending, especially to minority-, veteran-and women-owned businesses via radio, television, or electronic media.

For banks, Treasury implemented the SBLF program with supervisory consultation from the four federal banking regulators: FDIC, Federal Reserve, OCC, and OTS. After Treasury conducted an initial eligibility review for each applicant, Treasury requested that the regulators provide a supervisory consultation for eligible applicants, focusing on their financial condition and the results of the most recent examination. Regulators recorded their assessment in a Supervisory Consultation Memo to Treasury. For CDLFs, Treasury sought input from the Community Development Financial Institutions Fund, a bureau in Treasury that certifies these institutions.

SBLF Funding and Incentives for Small Business Lending

Under SBLF, Treasury can make capital investments in eligible institutions with total assets of less than $10 billion. Treasury provides institutions with capital by purchasing preferred stock or subordinated debt in each bank.[13,14] The amount of funding a institution could receive depended on its asset size as of the end of the fourth quarter of calendar year 2009. Specifically, if the qualifying bank had total assets of $1 billion or less, it could apply for SBLF funding that equals up to 5 percent of its risk-weighted assets (as reported in the call report immediately preceding the date of application).[15] If the qualifying bank had assets of more than $1 billion, but less than $10 billion, it could have applied for funding that equals up to 3 percent of its risk-weighted assets. The SBLF program also provides an option for eligible institutions to refinance preferred stock issued to the Treasury through TARP's CPP or CDCI. If the qualifying institution is a CPP or CDCI recipient, any capital that remains outstanding from these investments is deducted from the SBLF program limits. All CPP and CDCI outstanding amounts must be repaid when SBLF funding is received.

Participating banks must pay dividends or interest of 5 percent per year initially, with reduced rates available if they increase their small business lending. Specifically, the dividend rate payable will decrease as banks increase small business lending over their baselines. While the dividend rate will be no more than 5 percent for the first 2 years, a bank can reduce the rate to just 1 percent by generating a 10 percent increase in its lending to small businesses compared with its baseline. After 2 years, the dividend rate on the capital will increase to 7 percent if participating banks have not increased their small business lending and, after 4 1/2 years, the dividend rate on the capital will increase to 9 percent for all banks. For CDLFs, the initial dividend rate will be

2 percent for the first 8 years. After the eighth year, the rate will increase to 9 percent if the CDLF has not repaid the SBLF funding. This structure is designed to encourage CDLFs to repay the capital investment as soon as practicable. With the approval of its regulator, Treasury will allow SBLF participants to exit the program at any time simply by repaying the funding provided along with dividends owed for that period. Treasury requires that institutions that are participants in CPP or CDCI must increase their small business lending to receive a reduced dividend rate benefit from refinancing. Specifically, if a institution's business lending has not increased over its baseline (i.e., the amount that was outstanding in the four quarters ending June 30, 2010) amount by the ninth quarter, it will be required to pay a "lending incentive fee" equal to 2 percent per year on the total amount of outstanding SBLF funding.

Institutions chosen to participate in SBLF must submit an Initial Supplemental Report to Treasury that calculates the baseline level of small business lending and the initial dividend rate. SBLF institutions must continue submitting Quarterly Supplemental Reports to calculate dividend rates for the next quarter. The goal is to measure the institution's changes in qualified small business lending to determine changes, if any, to the dividend rate. In addition, SBLF institutions must complete a short annual lending survey and annual certifications to Treasury that attest the accuracy to the institutions' reports, among other things. In accordance with the act, Treasury plans to measure institutions' changes in qualified small business lending by the amount of loans outstanding each quarter against the baseline level.

TREASURY'S APPLICATION REQUIREMENTS AND DECISIONS WERE NOT ALWAYS TRANSPARENT

Treasury's Review Process Required Additional Steps to Evaluate Some Applicants

Treasury's process for evaluating SBLF applicants included several levels of review and input from multiple sources to help ensure that applicants were treated consistently and that banks approved for funding were financially viable and could repay the investments. Such procedures are an important control activity that helps ensure agency accountability over the use of government resources. Treasury's review focused primarily on the financial condition of applicants and drew not only on regulators' supervisory consultation, but also on an independent credit analysis of applicants' financial health—specifically, the likelihood that they would be able to repay SBLF investments and accompanying dividends—and to a lesser extent on the applicants' small business lending plans. Figure 1 provides an overview of the process for evaluating SBLF applicants.

First, Treasury checked whether applicants were eligible to participate in SBLF. For example, Treasury checked to make sure that the applicants had less than $10 billion in assets and were not on FDIC's problem bank list. Treasury also checked with the regulators to determine whether the applicants could pay dividends to Treasury, a process which we describe in more detail later. Furthermore, for applicants seeking to refinance their CPP or CDCI funds, Treasury checked to ensure that they had not missed more than one dividend payments under the program. The program office then entered applicants' information into a database.

Second, the Application Review Team considered various inputs for eligible applicants to help develop a preliminary recommendation to forward to the Investment Committee. According to Treasury, the Application Review Team included five members from Treasury with investment analysis experience to manage the application review process.[16] The inputs that the Application Review Team considered included the following:

- *Supervisory consultation memo:* As part of the evaluation process, Treasury obtained supervisory consultation from the appropriate federal banking regulators to determine the financial condition and performance of applicant banks. In the memo, the regulators did not recommend whether the applicant should be approved; rather the memo summarized supervisory information (e.g., CAMELS composite ratings and a description of material supervisory issues, if any) about the applicant's financial condition and performance and specifically indicated whether the applicant was viable.[17] "Viable" was defined as adequately capitalized, not expected to become undercapitalized, and not expected to be placed into conservatorship or receivership.[18]
- *Repayment probability:* The Application Review Team also considered an independent credit analysis of applicant's ability to repay SBLF investments while making consistent dividend payments to Treasury—which was referred to as the "repayment probability." Treasury hired financial agents to conduct this analysis. Using

publicly available information, these agents examined applicants' capital structure, asset quality, earnings capacity, and access to funding to develop a repayment probability estimate. According to Treasury officials, the purpose of the repayment probability analysis was to provide a forward-looking approach to help ensure that participants would generate enough future income to repay the SBLF investments and not solely rely on a determination of the applicant's financial condition information from their respective regulators. According to Treasury officials, the Application Review Team reviewed the repayment probability estimate and, if needed, updated the estimate to incorporate confidential supervisory information.

- *Sector analysis:* The Application Review Team reviewed sector analyses, on an as needed basis, on current industry trends and developments in the small bank credit sector because comparatively little market research was available. For example, some of the sector analyses included analysis of regional economies or summaries of important industry information, such as proposed regulatory and legislative changes. Treasury hired financial agents to perform the sector analysis.
- *Small business lending plans:* The Application Review Team summarized input from SBLF Program Office's evaluation of applicants' small business lending plans. The evaluation included the projected increase in small business lending, experience in small business lending, and plans to meet the needs of small businesses or provide appropriate outreach.[19]
- *Application Review Committee input:* The Application Review Team considered input from the Application Review Committee, which was made up of detailees from the FDIC, Federal Reserve, and OCC who were experienced in bank examinations.[20] Treasury established the Application Review Committee to further help ensure consistent treatment of bank applicants. The Application Review Committee was responsible for all bank applications that may have warranted additional review. For example, the Committee reviewed all applicants that receive a CAMELS composite rating of "3," had adverse performance ratios, or received inconsistent supervisory consultation from the relevant state and federal regulators.[21] In addition, the Application Review Committee took a "second look" at applicants deemed not viable by their respective regulators to ensure

that the supervisory consultation process had been applied consistently across bank applicants. Treasury said that it added this additional review by the Application Review Committee in response to a previous GAO recommendation.[22] The review process ends at this stage for applicants that the Application Review Committee did not recommend for further consideration and they are no longer considered for SBLF funding. According to Treasury, these decisions were further reviewed and affirmed by the Deputy Assistant Secretary.

Third, the Application Review Team then prepared a recommendation for the Investment Committee. The Investment Committee was a five-member body that included the SBLF Director (Chairman) and the Assistant Secretaries for Financial Institutions, Financial Markets, Economic Policy, and Management or their delegates. The Investment Committee was charged with reviewing and recommending applicants for funding and reviewed the information compiled by the Application Review Team to inform its recommendations. Applications recommended by the Investment Committee were presented for preliminary approval to the Deputy Assistant Secretary for Small Business, Community Development, and Affordable Housing Policy. After preliminary approval, the approved bank had 30 days to close the transaction.[23]

Because CDLFs are unregulated institutions, they do not face the same regulatory reporting requirements as banks and, because of differences in legislative requirements, Treasury developed a separate set of processes to evaluate their ability to meet the eligibility requirements and financial conditions. Treasury consulted with the CDFI fund to determine whether a CDLF applicant could receive SBLF funding on the basis of factors such as prior award history, compliance status, and certification requirements. To evaluate the CDLF's financial condition, Treasury hired a financial agent to perform a desk review and on-site visit to evaluate the CDLF's financial statements, risk management and control procedures, adequacy of information systems, and management structure. The Application Review Team considered these inputs and then made a funding recommendation for the Investment Committee. CDLF applicants recommended for approval by the Investment Committee were then provided to the Deputy Assistant Secretary for preliminary approval. Those that were not recommended were also reviewed and affirmed by the Deputy Assistant Secretary.

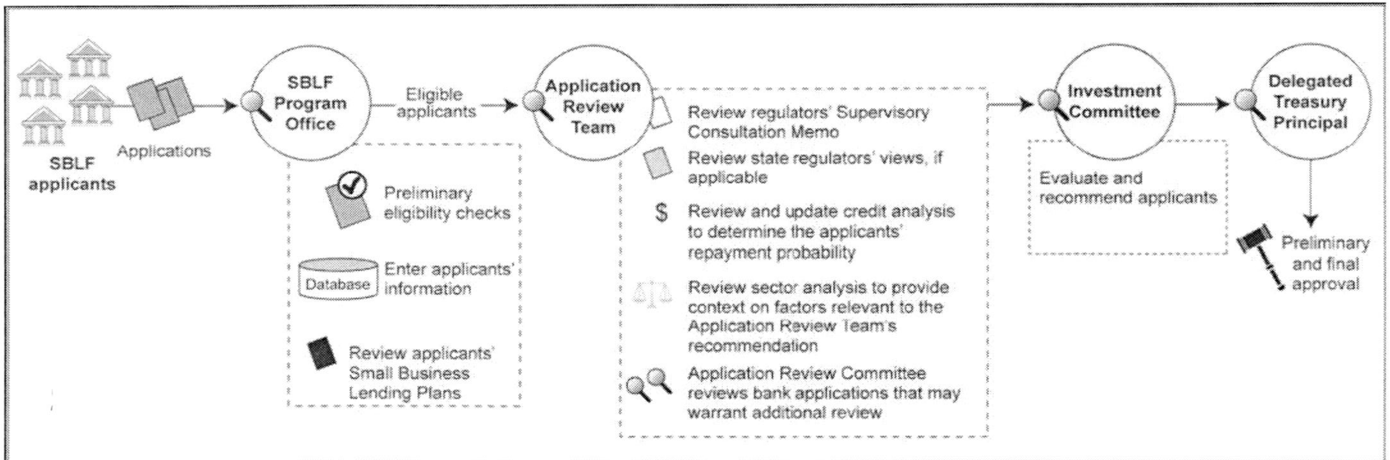

Sources: GAO analysis of Treasury information; Art Explosion (images).

Figure 1. Treasury's Process for Evaluating SBLF Applicants.

Our analysis of funding decisions found that Treasury generally followed its procedures, but we also identified some decisions that appeared to fall outside certain key parameters Treasury had established to guide its evaluation process. Treasury established specific parameters to evaluate SBLF applicants' financial conditions and, to a lesser extent, their small business lending plans. These parameters included that applicants should have at least an 80 percent probability of repayment and satisfactory performance ratios (e.g., nonperforming loan ratios of less than 40 percent, and construction and development loan ratios of less than 300 percent, Treasury's stated thresholds).[24] Treasury also considered the applicants' CAMELS composite ratings. For the evaluation criteria that we reviewed, we found the following for approved and nonapproved applicants:

- *Approved applicants.* Our review of Treasury data showed that 400 of the 935 applicants were approved. Treasury gave preliminary approval to a total of 400 SBLF applicants and funded 332. The remaining 68 of the approved applicants either chose not to participate in SBLF or were ultimately not approved because Treasury had evaluated updated information after they sent out the preliminary approval letter. All the approved applicants did not have restrictions on paying dividends. We also found that all approved applicants had CAMELS composite ratings of 1, 2, or 3 and had construction and development loan ratios of less than 300 percent. In addition, all but two approved applicants had what Treasury considered "responsive lending plans."[25] However, we found that 44 of the 400 (11 percent) approved applicants had an initial calculation of repayment probability of less than 80 percent. The lowest repayment probability estimate for an approved bank was 48 percent. In addition, we found that 13 of the 400 (3.2 percent) approved applicants had nonperforming loan ratios (as a percentage of capital and loan loss reserves) greater than 40 percent (based on first quarter 2011 data).[26]
- *Nonapproved applicants.* Our analysis showed that, out of 935 applicants, a total of 535 applicants were not approved.[27] Fifty-three of the nonapproved applicants were not eligible based on Treasury's initial eligibility check. Of the nonapproved applicants, 175 applicants considered viable by their respective regulator(s) and able to pay dividends were ultimately not approved.[28] Of these nonapproved applicants, 85 (48.6 percent) had a CAMELS composite rating of 2, and 49 (28 percent) had both a CAMELS composite rating of 2 and an

initial calculation of repayment probability of higher than 80 percent.[29]

To examine the decisions that appeared to fall outside of Treasury's stated parameters in more depth, we judgmentally selected 15 applicants that appeared to be particularly out of line with Treasury's evaluation parameters. As part of this analysis, we reviewed minutes from the Application Review Committee and Investment Committee and interviewed Treasury officials. According to Treasury, these committees had the flexibility to consider all factors—supervisory information, financial data, as well as repayment probability—relating to the applicants' financial health in making their decisions. For 12 of the 15 applicants, the Investment Committee's minutes and other documents provided additional explanation for their decisions. In particular, Treasury's Investment Committee minutes generally indicated that the financial agent's probability estimate was deemed too conservative for the approved applicants with repayment probabilities of less than 80 percent because, for example, the estimates did not include confidential supervisory information. For the remaining three applicants, Treasury officials were able to explain the rationale for their decisions—for example, we learned that the Application Review Committee or Investment Committee discussed concerns about the applicants' financial condition, but these concerns were not clearly documented in the committees' minutes. Treasury officials were able to clarify their decisions in subsequent conversations with us. Specifically, 2 nonapproved applicants from the 15 applicants that we reviewed in more depth were deemed viable by their regulators, were able to pay dividends, and had a 96 percent repayment probability. However, the Application Review Committee did not recommend that these applicants go forward and the committee's minutes documented that both applicants had asset quality problems. Treasury officials further explained that financial agents estimated a high repayment probability for these applicants but lacked access to certain confidential supervisory information that would have lowered the repayment probability estimates. In particular, the financial agent projected a low level of losses, but the Application Review Team estimated that the applicants could have a higher level of losses based on confidential supervisory information about the applicants' classified assets—a measure of assets with well-defined weaknesses that jeopardize the liquidation of debts.

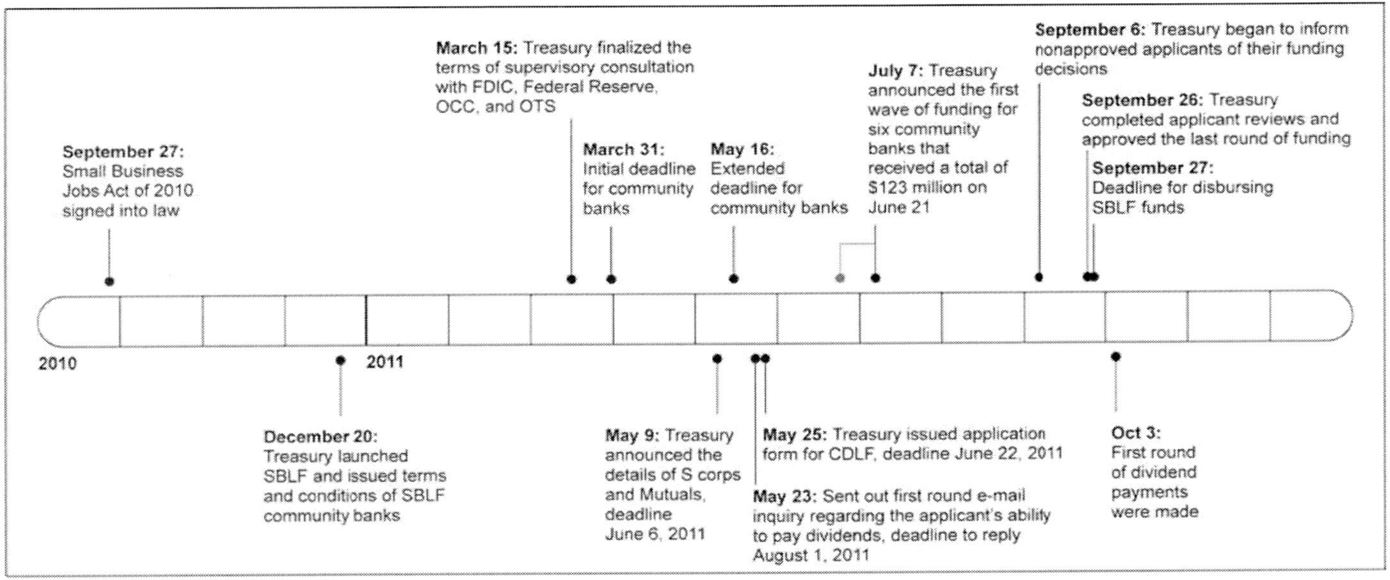

Source: GAO.

Figure 2. Timeline for the Implementation of SBLF, September 2010 through October 2011.

Treasury officials acknowledged that the initial repayment probability provided by the financial agents did not reflect regulators' views of the financial condition of the banks, especially confidential information concerning adversely classified assets. According to Treasury officials, this was due to the financial agents' reliance on only publicly available information to develop the repayment probability. Therefore, additional steps were taken to revise the estimates in certain cases. Treasury officials explained that the Application Review Team updated the probability estimate with confidential supervisory information in certain cases to help inform Investment Committee's evaluations. While these updated repayment probability estimates were considered, they were not recorded in Treasury's database. However, Treasury officials explained that this updated information was typically included in either the Application Review Team's recommendation memorandum to the Investment Committee or the Investment Committee minutes.[30]

Time to Review Applications Was Affected by Implementation Challenges and Funding Deadline

Treasury faced multiple delays in implementing the SBLF program and disbursing SBLF funds by the statutory deadline of September 27, 2011. Treasury launched the program in December 2010 and had initially intended to start approving applications by mid-January 2011 and begin closing the application window by early April 2011. However, Treasury extended the application deadline for community banks from March 31 to May 16, 2001. In addition, Treasury did not begin the application process for banks that were S Corps and Mutuals and CDLFs until May 12, 2011, and set application deadlines for these institutions for June 6, 2011, and June 22, 2011, respectively. Because of these implementation delays, Treasury did not disburse any funds until the end of June 2011, and finished approving the applicants on September 26, 2011, a day before the funding deadline (see figure 2).

Treasury officials said that they encountered a number of implementation challenges that delayed the disbursement of SBLF funds. First, the need to develop SBLF's infrastructure, including hiring staff and contractors, contributed to delays in starting the applicant review process. Second, Treasury officials noted that while they wanted to expeditiously disburse the funds, they were committed to developing and implementing a robust set of internal controls, which can take time. Third, negotiations over the regulators' role in reviewing SBLF applicants for investments took much longer than anticipated, and an agreement was not reached until March 2011. According to Treasury, this delay resulted from differing views among the federal regulators—FDIC, Federal Reserve, OCC, and OTS—about whether they should make recommendations to Treasury. Ultimately, the regulators and Treasury agreed that the regulators would not be required to make recommendations on whether the applicant should be approved for SBLF but instead would document their analyses of SBLF applicant's financial condition and performance and determination of the applicant's viability in the Supervisory Consultation Memo to inform Treasury's evaluation.[31] Treasury also agreed to protect the privacy of the confidential supervisory information the regulators provided through a memorandum of understanding or similar letter agreements.

Treasury also reconsidered applicants that had not been approved upon their initial review through September, when new supervisory information became available. Treasury officials explained that they continued to receive updated supervisory information from regulators through September, often because some banks had gone through a more recent examination. Treasury officials wanted to reevaluate the nonapproved bank applicants using this updated information to ensure that these applicants were fully considered. Therefore, Treasury delayed making final decisions for some applicants so that updated supervisory information could be considered. According to Treasury officials, waiting for such information proved beneficial for 18 applicants that were ultimately approved to participate in SBLF.

Lack of Clarity about Program Requirements and Transparency of Some Decisions Created Confusion

Treasury did not explicitly explain to applicants all SBLF program requirements at the beginning of the application period and did not inform nonapproved applicants of their status in a timely manner, which created confusion among applicants. Treasury initiated several outreach efforts to educate the public and potential applicants about SBLF. These efforts included a website with background and guidance on the program and frequently asked questions. Treasury also established a call center to respond to inquiries from interested institutions and held several webinars to explain the program. However, these communication efforts were not sufficient to address unexpected developments and the delays in the program. Furthermore, Treasury's communication strategy did not appear to be effective in communicating with external stakeholders such as the banking regulators, industry associations, and Congress. Two key developments illustrate these weaknesses.

Program Requirements and Dividend Restrictions

Treasury did not clearly explain one of the program requirements to SBLF applicants—that they needed to be able to pay dividends on SBLF funds they received—during the application process, leading to confusion among many applicants about the program. After the application deadline for banks, Treasury realized that the information from federal regulators would not necessarily indicate whether banks had dividend restrictions. For example, dividend restrictions may come from state regulators and the applicant's own board of directors and, therefore, would not be reflected in the federal regulators' supervisory information.[32] To obtain this information, in May 2011, Treasury sent applicants an e-mail asking them to fill out a new form about their ability to pay dividends. In its request, Treasury did not explain that this was not a new requirement.

According to industry representatives, many banks had not realized that demonstrating their ability to pay dividends was a requirement for eligibility and, therefore, viewed Treasury's request for information on dividend restriction as a new requirement that was added subsequent to the application process. These representatives noted that the requirement that participants be able to pay dividends was not explicitly communicated when the information on SBLF was first posted on SBLF's website in December 2010.[33] For example, it was not included in the initial guidance, the application form, or the question-and-answer section on the website. This program requirement was also not mentioned in Treasury's initial outreach efforts (e.g., webinars and conferences). Similarly, officials from FDIC, Federal Reserve, and OCC also told us that Treasury's decision to not fund banks with dividend restrictions had not been explicitly stated when the program was established in December 2010. In addition, the regulators noted that Treasury officials did not discuss this issue with them until early May 2011.

Treasury officials noted that the requirement was described in the program's published Summary of Preferred Terms posted on December 20, 2010, and was not a new eligibility criterion or policy change. Specifically, Treasury officials pointed out that the summary of terms stated that the main policy instrument for SBLF was the dividend rate, which would be an incentive for institutions to lend to small businesses and repay SBLF funding within a certain time frame. Given the program's focus on the dividend rate, Treasury officials assumed that applicants would understand that they needed to be free of restrictions on paying dividends.

The confusion about the dividend restriction program requirement resulted in a number of banks unable to currently pay dividends applying for the program. Specifically, our analysis showed that 231 of the applicants had some form of dividend restrictions.[34] According to industry representatives we spoke with, if Treasury had communicated this requirement more clearly from the outset, banks might not have spent time and effort applying to the program or would have had more time to work with their regulators on lifting the restrictions to increase their chances of being accepted.

Status of Applications

Although approved institutions began receiving funds in June 2011, many applicants that were not selected to participate in SBLF were not told of their status until September 2011, almost 4 months after the application deadline. Treasury officials explained that by waiting to make final decisions for some applicants that would not receive approval on the basis of results from the first-quarter call reports, Treasury was able to consider results from the second-quarter call reports that contained data on the banks' financial conditions through June 2011.

When Treasury informed applicants of their status, it did not initially communicate why the banks were not approved. This lack of information created confusion and frustration among some applicants. For instance, representatives from one banking trade group told us that some members were confused about not being approved because they had high CAMELS composite ratings and no dividend restrictions and their respective regulators had informed them that they had received a positive viability determination. As we noted earlier, our analysis of Treasury's funding decisions found some applicants that fell within the established parameters but were not approved. Specifically, we found 85 applicants that were not approved by Treasury despite (1) receiving a positive viability determination, (2) having a CAMELS composite rating of 2, and (3) being able to pay dividends. Treasury officials told us that they did not initially explain to the applicants as to why they were not approved because relevant supervisory information was confidential, and Treasury was prohibited by law from disclosing this information. However, according to OCC, they were also not initially consulted about Treasury's decision about what to communicate to applicants who were denied, and when such discussions did take place, OCC encouraged Treasury to provide explanations to applicants. In addition, FDIC and the Federal Reserve noted that the regulator's confidential information was only one input into Treasury's decision-making process, and the investment decisions were Treasury's, not the regulators. Nevertheless, Treasury's emphasis on the confidential supervisory information contributed to the delay in notifying applicants of the reasons for not being approved and reduced the transparency of the decisions. Treasury informed us that they have subsequently reached an agreement with the regulators to share more information on those decisions with the affected SBLF applicants and has finished contacting nonapproved applicants with additional information regarding its decision.

Treasury's ineffective communication about the dividend restriction program requirement, delays in communicating the status of applicantions, and lack of explanation for its nonapproval decisions resulted in confusion among applicants and may also have negatively affected how the potential pool of applicants and the public perceived the program. Federal government internal control standards state that management should ensure that the agency has adequate means of communicating with and obtaining information from external stakeholders when such information could have a significant impact on the agency's achieving its goals.[35] The experience and lessons from the first year implementing SBLF could be instructive to Treasury's communication strategy about the status of the program going forward. Without a more effective communication strategy that enhances understanding of the program's goals and requirements and recognizes the need for timely communication with external stakeholders, SBLF will continue to be poorly understood by the public and Congress.

CHARACTERISTICS OF APPLICANTS AND PARTICIPANTS AND FACTORS AFFECTING SBLF PARTICIPATION

Fewer institutions applied to SBLF and received funding than initially anticipated. Although SBLF's authorizing legislation provided up to $30 billion for investing, Treasury expected program participation to be lower and budgeted $17.4 billion in SBLF investments in its fiscal year 2011 budget request, based on an internal analysis of projected program activity.[36] However, interest in SBLF was lower than Treasury anticipated, with 935 financial institutions applying to the program for a combined funding request of $11.7 billion. Ultimately, 332 institutions received $4.03 billion in SBLF investments. Of the 332 program participants, 281 (85 percent) were banks, while the remaining 51 institutions (15 percent) were CDLFs.

The program attracted smaller institutions including those seeking to refinance CPP and CDCI funds. Sixty-five percent (612) of SBLF applicants were small institutions with total assets of $500 million or less, and 61 percent (204) of participants fall within this category.[37] In addition, about one-third (320) of the total number of applicants were seeking to refinance CPP and CDCI funds, and these applicants requested $6.7 billion in funds—representing about 57 percent of the total dollar amount requested (see figure 3). Treasury approved 137 of the applicants seeking to refinance CPP and CDCI funds, investing a total of $2.7 billion in these institutions. This represented about 67 percent of all SBLF investments.

The program also attracted institutions from across the country. Figure 4 shows the geographic distribution of SBLF investments by number of institutions per state and SBLF dollars per state. The Small Business Jobs Act required the Secretary of Treasury to consider, among other factors, increasing opportunities for small business development in high unemployment areas—a consideration Treasury sought to address by focusing outreach activities in 10 states with the highest unemployment (as well as the District of Columbia), which included direct outbound calling efforts to eligible institutions in these states. We found that higher levels of state unemployment were not associated with greater SBLF funding in the state.[38]

Comparison of SBLF Applicants and Banks to Non-SBLF Peer Banks

To better put the financial characteristics of SBLF applicant and participant banks in context and to describe the types of institutions that were attracted to and funded by SBLF, we generated a group of peer institutions that had not applied to SBLF and compared them with SBLF applicants and participants (funded banks), in addition to comparing SBLF participants with applicants that were not funded.[39] For example, SBLF participants had lower capital ratios and a smaller proportion of certain small business loans (as a percentage of total domestic business and farm loans) than the peer group. Participants also had higher asset quality than peers.

- *Capital ratios.* Both SBLF applicants and participants had less capital than their nonapplicant peers. The risk-based capital ratio—the ratio of total capital to risk-weighted assets—was about 15 percent for both SBLF applicants and participants, compared with roughly 19 percent for peers.[40]
- *Small loan portfolio.* Both SBLF applicants and participants had a smaller proportion of certain small loans on their balance sheets—that is, loans of less than $1 million for business and commercial real estate and less than $500,000 for farms—than nonapplicants.[41] For SBLF applicants small loans on average comprised 57 percent of loans, whereas participants had an average of 56 percent. For peer banks, the average was 62 percent.
- *Asset quality.* SBLF participants compared more favorably to applicants that were not funded and their peers in asset quality. Problem loans, a measure of asset quality, averaged 2.5 percent for SBLF participants compared with 5.7 percent for applicants that were not funded and 3.8 percent for peers.
- *CAMELS composite ratings.* On average, SBLF participants also had better CAMELS composite ratings than applicants that were not funded. SBLF banks averaged a CAMELS composite rating of 2.0, while applicants that were not funded averaged a CAMELS rating of 2.7, indicating some areas of supervisory concern. Nonapplicant peers had an average CAMELS composite rating of 2.1.[42]

Banks Frequently Cited Lack of Demand as the Most Important Reason for Not Applying to the Program

In our nationally representative survey of banks, about four-fifths responded that they did not apply or plan to apply to the SBLF program.[43] The most important reason cited for not applying to the SBLF program was little or no anticipated demand for small business credit followed closely by a preference not to participate in government programs, as shown in figure 5. The banks that did apply anticipated loan demand in their respective areas, but indicated that their most important reason for applying was because SBLF was a source of capital to meet a growing demand for small business credit (as shown in figure 5). Other reasons for applying to SBLF were that the program's cost of capital was more attractive relative to market alternatives and that the program offered the option of refinancing CPP/CDCI funds.

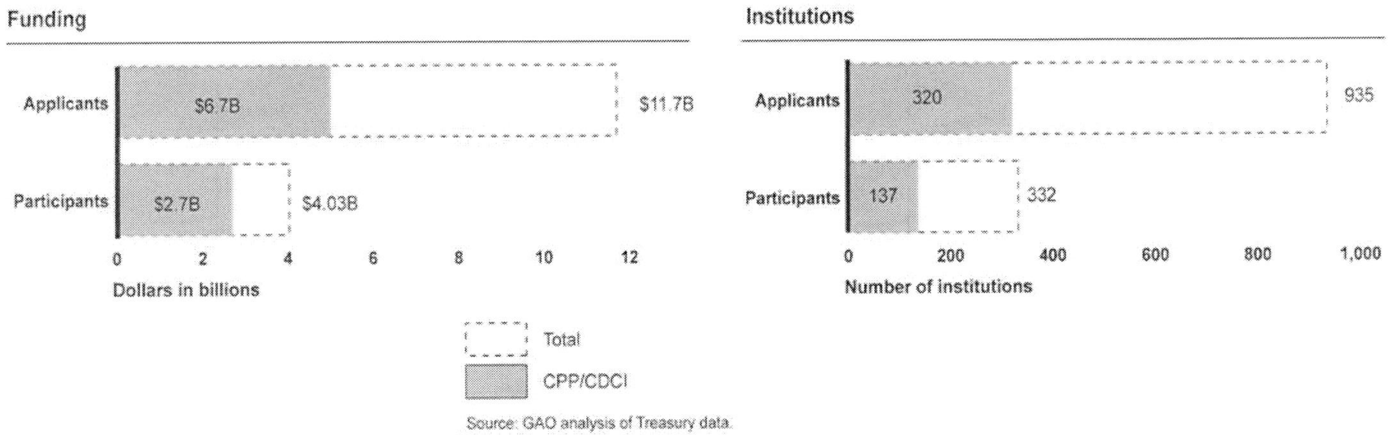

Note: Of the $6.7 billion in requested to refinance CPP and CDCI funds, $5.69 billion was to repay CPP/CDCI principal. $2.2 billion of the ultimate $2.7 billion CPP/CDCI investments were for refinancing outstanding CPP and CDCI funds.

Figure 3. SBLF Applicant and Participant Data.

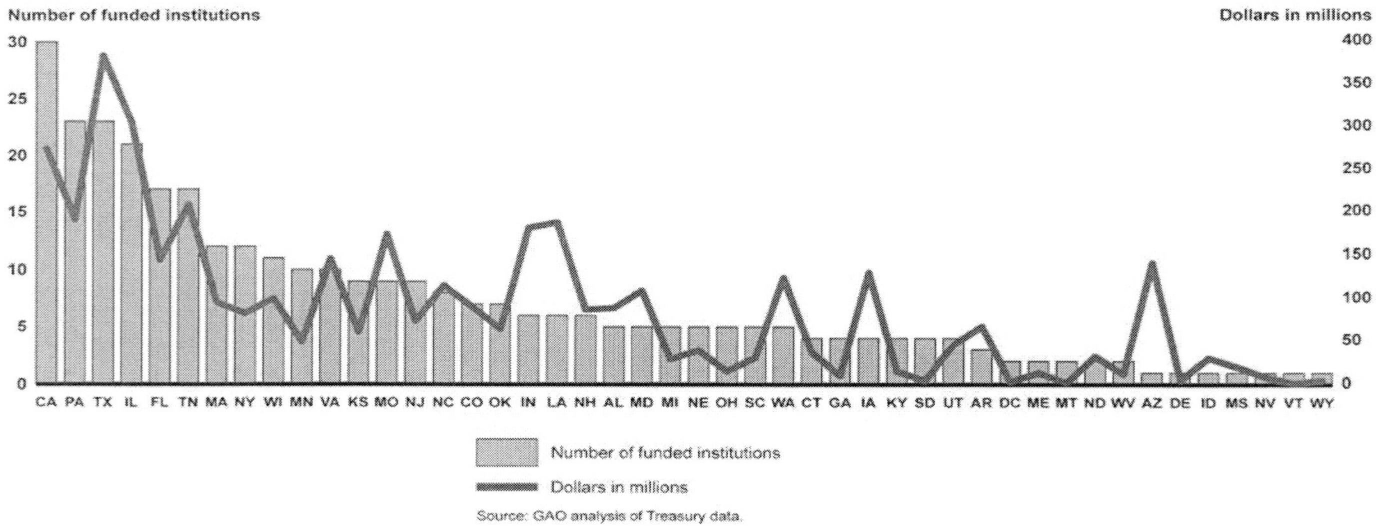

Note: Five states did not have institutions that received SBLF funds: Alaska, Hawaii, New Mexico, Oregon, and Rhode Island.

Figure 4. SBLF Investments by State.

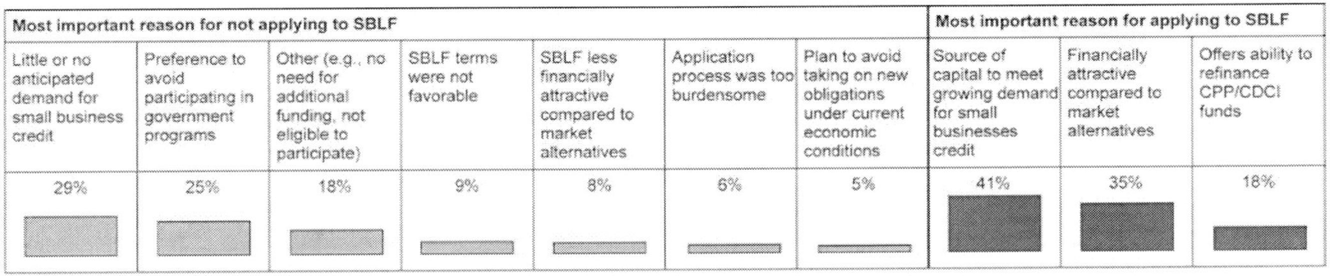

Source: GAO survey results.

Note: The 95 percent confidence intervals around the estimates for not applying to the SBLF do not exceed plus or minus 5 percentage points. The 95 percent confidence intervals around the estimates for applying to the SBLF do not exceed plus or minus 12 percentage points.

Figure 5. Factors Affecting Banks' Participation in SBLF.

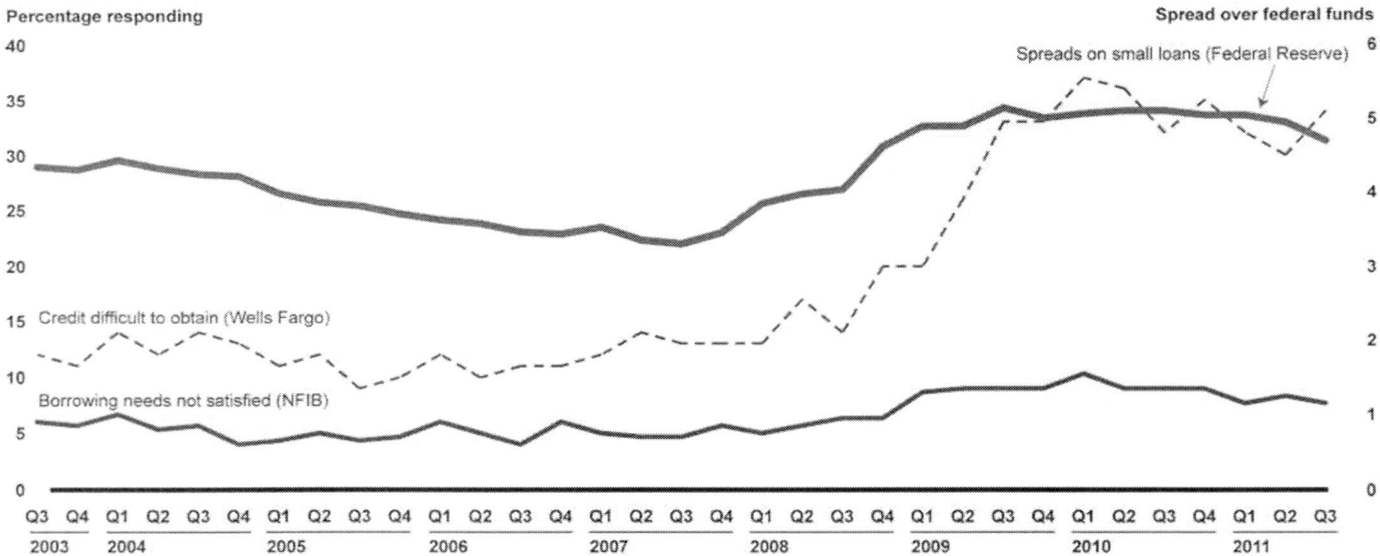

Source: GAO analysis of Wells Fargo, National Federation of Independent Business, and Federal Reserve data.

Note: The indicators in the figure and the organizations that measure them are the following: (1) the National Federation of Independent Business, a small business trade association, surveys its members on whether or not their borrowing needs have been satisfied; (2) Wells Fargo conducts a survey of small business with a sample constructed by Gallup and Dun & Bradstreet; and (3) the Federal Reserve surveys banks on the price of credit for loans of various sizes.

Figure 6. Indicators of Small Business Credit Conditions, Third Quarter 2003-Third Quarter 2011.

Treasury Has Not Finalized Plans to Monitor SBLF Participants or Track SBLF's Impact

Credit Conditions Remain Challenging for Small Businesses

The SBLF program was designed to improve small businesses' access to credit, which had become difficult to obtain since 2008. We examined trends in the credit markets from late 2003 through the third quarter of 2011 to document the credit market environment in which the program and its participants must operate. As shown in figure 6, from the second half of 2003 through early 2008, credit conditions were stable and credit was relatively easy to obtain. Credit became increasingly difficult to obtain (tight) from 2008 through 2009 in the midst of the financial crisis, and it peaked between mid-2009 and mid-2010. Credit availability has eased somewhat since its peak.

Other indicators that we reviewed also demonstrate easier access to credit since the 2007-2009 financial crisis. According to a Federal Reserve survey of relatively large banks, more banks began easing than tightening standards for loans to small firms starting in the third quarter of 2010. Further, lending to small businesses began increasing in the second half of 2009, according to a measure of loan originations.[44] While credit availability has eased since 2009, movement in each indicator of small business lending has been volatile in the last few years, and small business credit remains tight relative to historical averages. However, a return to credit conditions of the boom years prior to the financial crisis would not necessarily be expected. Although small business credit conditions have improved since the 2007-2009 financial crisis, uncertainty about future credit conditions and the economic outlook increases the importance of monitoring SBLF participants going forward.

Treasury Has Not Finalized Plans for Monitoring SBLF Participants and the Program's Impact Because Focus Has Been on Implementation

Treasury has not finalized plans to monitor SBLF participants. Treasury officials acknowledged the need for ongoing analysis, monitoring, and reporting on SBLF participants, but at this time only has some procedures in place and preliminary plans for other procedures. These plans include potentially hiring outside firms to assist in managing the $4.03 billion SBLF portfolio, using such firms to evaluate the financial data that SBLF institutions provide, and developing a system to detect inconsistent or inaccurate information that might be submitted in participants' quarterly supplemental reports. Treasury has taken some steps toward monitoring and reporting on SBLF participants. For example, in October 2011, Treasury began publishing, on its website, SBLF transaction reports that include dividend payment information. These reports include, among other things, all SBLF participants, the dividend payments expected and received, and total payments to date.

Similarly, Treasury has not finalized plans to assess the impact of the SBLF program. Treasury is required to provide a written report to Congress on a quarterly basis that includes information about how participating institutions have used the SBLF funds they received. Treasury officials stated that their plans for assessing impact are still being developed. However, Treasury officials told us that they have some preliminary plans, including tracking the number of small business loans using data from SBLF participants' quarterly supplemental reports in order to gauge increased small business lending; conducting an annual survey of small business lending; and conducting a study on how women- and minority-owned small businesses have been impacted by the program. Treasury officials have also considered comparing SBLF banks and a non-SBLF bank peer group to identify any relationships between the program and small business lending. Officials noted that they are still considering various approaches for how to assess the program's impact, including how to collect and report needed data. In addition, Treasury officials acknowledged particular difficulties associated with linking SBLF to growth in employment, including how to account for the role of loans in keeping businesses operating that might otherwise have shut down, and how to treat loan refinancing.

Treasury officials told us that they have not finalized their plans for monitoring SBLF participants or assessing the impact of the program because they have been focused on implementing the program. As discussed, Treasury was evaluating applicants and making funding decisions through most of September. While Treasury officials said they recognize the importance of such assessments, they stated that they have not had sufficient time to devote to fully developing their plans.

Treasury faces a number of challenges as it moves forward in finalizing long-term plans to monitor SBLF participants and evaluate the SBLF program. First, Treasury will likely need to monitor SBLF participants without direct input from the federal regulators. According to Federal Reserve, OCC, and FDIC officials, there are currently no plans to coordinate with Treasury in monitoring SBLF banks. Regulators noted that their role, as defined by the statute, was to provide input to Treasury about the banks' financial viability during the application process. The statute does not give the regulators a role in monitoring SBLF banks, and regulators stated that SBLF banks will not be treated differently or have their own set of exam procedures during their supervisory examinations. One agency noted that they will review bank lending practices as part of the regular examination process. Second, the relationship between small business lending and job growth is complex, and making conclusions about the impact of the program on employment based on lending at SBLF banks will not be straightforward. Third, while using a control group to assess performance is a best practice, any assessment could be complicated by the fact the SBLF banks will report their small business lending in a way that is inconsistent with call reports of non-SBLF banks (the peer group). For example, as noted earlier, SBLF considers small loans to be those under $10 million, whereas the call reports collect data on loans under $1 million (or under $500,000 in the case of farm-related loans). Without comparable data for peers, measuring the impact it of SBLF on small business credit availability will be difficult.

Internal control standards for the federal government state that internal control activities are a major part of efficiently and effectively managing a program.[45] Control activities, such as (1) proper execution of transactions and events, (2) accurate and timely recording of transactions and events, (3) and establishing and reviewing performance measures, are an integral part of an agency's planning, implementing, reviewing, and accountability for stewardship of government resources and achieving effective results. Establishing performance measures and developing a process for monitoring participating financial institutions will be critical to identifying and addressing any potential problems in these institutions' compliance with program requirements.[46] Until Treasury finalizes its plans for monitoring compliance and assessing impact in a timely manner, it will not be positioned to anticipate and manage payment problems and other program risks. For example, if the macroeconomic conditions deteriorate, SBLF participants may not have as many opportunities to lend to small businesses as originally planned, and participants may be obliged to pay a higher dividend rate than they originally anticipated. Participants may also need to preserve their capital and thus may be unable to pay dividends or their respective regulators may restrict their ability to do so if their condition warrants such a restriction, for example, if economic conditions deteriorate sufficiently. Furthermore, SBLF participants may loosen their underwriting standards to meet higher lending targets, a concern shared by OCC. Such factors will also need to be considered as Treasury develops its plans for monitoring and assessing the impact of the SBLF program. Until Treasury's plans are finalized and implemented, it will not be able to provide information on the effectiveness of the SBLF program.[47]

CONCLUSION

Intended to improve the flow of credit to small businesses, the SBLF program attracted fewer banks and community development loan funds than expected and encountered significant delays in providing funding. Instances of poor communication during the first year of the SBLF program created confusion among applicants. Although Treasury conducted numerous outreach efforts to inform potential applicants and the public about the program, some communications were incomplete or unclear. Specifically, Treasury did not initially make clear that participants would have to be free of restrictions on paying dividends, and more than 200 applicants that could not make such payments applied to the program without knowing that they would not meet program requirements. Moreover, Treasury did not explain to applicants its reasons for not accepting them in the SBLF program, and many of these applicants did not find out that they had not been approved until months after applying. Treasury later took steps to improve communications by working with the bank regulators to determine how to communicate to banks the reasons for not being approved. However, the experience of SBLF applicants highlights the importance of timely, transparent communications throughout the program implementation process, a lesson that will continue to be important going forward.

SBLF's impact on small business lending will be difficult to measure, both because Treasury has yet to finalize evaluation plans and because multiple factors affect lending trends. Treasury has not fully developed procedures to monitor participants for compliance with the program's requirements or measures to assess SBLF's effectiveness in increasing small business lending. Establishing procedures is an important component of accountability for stewardship of government resources. As we found in reviewing Treasury's application evaluation process, procedures also may need to adapt to changing circumstances, and such adjustments should be clearly documented. Monitoring compliance, including compliance with program terms such as dividend payments, and taking steps to ensure that the data participants provide on their small business lending are accurate, is important going forward. In addition, the reports on small business lending will be an important component of measuring the effectiveness of SBLF. Efforts to measure SBLF's impact will be difficult because many factors affect trends in small business and other lending. In addition, limited participation in the program highlights the challenge of balancing the need to protect taxpayer interests with the desire to distribute SBLF funds to struggling areas of the economy. Treasury's efforts to consider approaches for isolating the impact of SBLF will be critical to providing a rigorous assessment of whether the program is effective. While Treasury officials said that they had been unable to complete plans to monitor compliance and assess SBLF's impact on small business lending during the application and initial disbursement process, now is the time for Treasury to finalize its plans for monitoring compliance and assessing SBLF. Without a thorough assessment of the SBLF program's performance, Congress and other policymakers will lack important information about the effectiveness of capital infusion programs for increasing small business lending.

RECOMMENDATIONS FOR EXECUTIVE ACTION

While Treasury took steps to evaluate SBLF applicants in a consistent manner and provide information about the program through numerous outreach efforts, we recommend that the Secretary of the Treasury take the following three additional actions going forward:

- To promote transparency and improve communication with SBLF participants and other interested stakeholders, such as Congress and the bank regulators, Treasury should apply lessons learned from the application review phase of SBLF to help improve its communication strategy going forward.
- To enhance the transparency and accountability of the SBLF program, Treasury should finalize (1) procedures for monitoring participants, including procedures to ensure that Treasury is receiving accurate information on participants' small business lending and (2) plans for assessing the performance of the SBLF program, including measures that can isolate the impact of SBLF from other factors that affect small business lending.

Agency Comments and Our Evaluation

We provided a draft of this report to Treasury, FDIC, Federal Reserve, and OCC for review and comment. Treasury provided written comments. In its comments, Treasury agreed with our three recommendations and stated it is taking steps to incorporate these recommendations into existing plans and procedures to further support transparency and accountability. Treasury noted that it has worked to achieve a high level of transparency and accountability throughout the implementation of the SBLF program. For example, Treasury stated that it had conducted extensive outreach with potential applicants, including participating in industry events, teleconferences, and webinars. Treasury also provided technical comments, which we incorporated as appropriate. In addition, FDIC, Federal Reserve, and OCC provided technical comments, which we incorporated as appropriate.

A. Nicole Clowers
Director
Financial Markets and Community Investment

Appendix I. Objectives, Scope, and Methodology

The objectives of our report were to examine (1) the procedures that the Department of the Treasury (Treasury) developed to implement SBLF and evaluate applications for Small Business Lending Fund (SBLF) funds; (2) the characteristics of institutions applying to and receiving SBLF funds and the factors that may have influenced banks' decision to participate; and (3) Treasury's plans to monitor SBLF participants and measure the SBLF's progress in increasing small business lending.

To assess Treasury's evaluation process for SBLF applications, we reviewed Treasury's policies, procedures, and internal controls for SBLF, including nonpublic documents, such as the Treasury's internal control procedures and Application Review Committee and Investment Committee minutes, and publicly available material from the SBLF website. We reviewed Treasury's and the four federal regulators' respective roles and responsibilities with respect to evaluating applicants and compared them with the same roles for the Capital Purchase Program (CPP), a capital infusion program under the Troubled Asset Relief Program (TARP) that is similar to SBLF. We interviewed officials from Treasury, Federal Deposit Insurance Corporation (FDIC), Board of Governors of the Federal Reserve System (Federal Reserve), the Office of the Comptroller of the Currency (OCC), and the Office of Thrift Supervision (OTS) to obtain information on their SBLF applicant evaluation processes and to discuss the similarities and differences between SBLF and CPP in terms of their roles and the processes for evaluating applicants. We also interviewed representatives of industry trade groups, including American Bankers' Association, International Franchise Association National Federation of Independent Business, Independent Community Bankers Association, and the National Association of Government Guaranteed Lenders to obtain their perspectives on SBLF and the application process.

To identify applicants that fell outside of Treasury's stated evaluation parameters, we obtained data from Treasury, FDIC and SNL Financial (SNL) for all applicants on key inputs that Treasury used to inform its funding decisions, including CAMELS composite ratings, repayment probability, performance ratios, lending plan scores, dividend restriction information, and results of regulators' financial viability assessments. To assess the reliability of Treasury's data, we (1) performed electronic checking for errors in accuracy and completeness; (2) reviewed related documentation, such as minutes from the Application Review Committee and Investment Committee; and (3) held numerous meetings and remained in ongoing correspondence with Treasury to discuss data fields, analysis procedures, and weekly data updates. When we found inconsistencies, for example, between the weekly data updates or between the data and published information, we clarified them with Treasury. For example, during our interviews with Treasury, we learned that 60 applicants were approved by Treasury but did not close and were labeled in the same category ("withdrawn") as applicants that were not approved. After clarifying and resolving our questions pertaining to the data, we concluded that the updated data set was reliable for the purpose of identifying applicants that fell outside of Treasury's stated evaluation parameters.

Using this updated and corrected data set, we performed an analysis for all 935 applicants to identify which of the applicants, both approved and nonapproved, fell out of Treasury's stated evaluation parameters (Table 1 lists the key data that Treasury used to inform its funding decisions and their corresponding parameters). We compared all data fields pertaining to Treasury's stated evaluation parameters, such as the regulator's viability assessment, repayment probability estimates, and lending plan results to Treasury's decision data field to identify those applicants outside of the parameters. We did not review the evaluation documents, such as regulator's supervisory consultation memos and minutes from the Application Review and Investment Committees for all 935 applicants.

Table 1. Main Parameters Treasury Used for Evaluating

SBLF Applicants

Key Data	Parameters
Eligibility	Treasury determined only all approved applicants must first pass the initial eligibility check .
Positive financial viability	Treasury determined only all approved applicants must first receive a positive financial viability assessment from their respective regulators.
CAMELS composite ratings[a]	Treasury considered CAMELS composite ratings of 1, 2 or 3 as acceptable. Per the legislation, problem banks (i.e., banks with CAMELS composite ratings of 4 and 5) were not eligible.
Repayment probability estimate	Treasury determined that repayment probability of 80 percent as the minimum acceptable. An initial estimate was developed by financial agents. Treasury reviewed this initial estimate and, if needed, updated the estimate to incorporate confidential supervisory information.
Key performance ratios	Treasury considers the following as thresholds that would require further review: • *Classified assets ratio:* Classified assets/Net Tier 1 capital + allowance for loan and lease losses (ALLL): greater than 100 percent[b] • *Nonperforming loans ratio:* Nonperforming loans (NPLS) + other real estate owned (OREO) /Net Tier 1 capital + ALLL: greater than 40 percent • *Construction and development loans:* Construction and development loans/Total risk-based capital: greater than 300 percent[c]
Lending plan scores	Treasury evaluated the lending plans as either responsive or nonresponsive. Treasury rated applicants' lending plan based on a 12 point evaluation. Any applicants that received 8 points or above, their lending plans were deemed responsive. The ones that received 7 points or below were deemed nonresponsive.
Dividend restrictions	Treasury determined only applicants that are able to pay dividends to SBLF funds could be approved.

Source: GAO summary of Treasury documentation.

[a] This exclude CDLFs, because CDLFs do not face the same regulatory reporting requirements as banks and thus do not have supervisory data.

[b] Tier 1 capital is considered the most stable and readily available capital for supporting a bank's operations. It covers core capital elements, such as common stockholder's equity and noncumulative perpetual preferred stock.

[c] Classified assets are known only by the regulators, so the financial agents would not be able to do this in the absence of the supervisory consultation memos. The "allowance for loan and lease losses" (ALLL) is an account maintained by financial institutions to cover incurred losses in their loan and lease portfolios. The "other real estate owned" (OREO) is an account used for examination and reporting purposes that primarily includes real estate owned by a financial institution as a result of foreclosure.

Using the results from this analysis, we then selected a small, nongeneralizable sample of 15 applicants that appeared to be particularly out of line with Treasury's stated parameters for additional review. In selecting the sample, we attempted to identify at least 3 applicants from each of the following categories:

- 6 approved outliers that had a repayment probability of less than 63 percent
- 3 nonapproved applicants that had a repayment probability of greater than 95 percent
- 3 approved outliers that had nonperforming loan ratios of greater than 55 percent
- 3 nonapproved applicants that had a no nonperforming loans

Because our findings are based on a nongeneralizable sample, they cannot be generalized to all applicants. However, because they represent significant deviations from Treasury's stated evaluation parameters, our analysis provides useful examples of how Treasury used these inputs in making funding decisions. As part of this analysis, we reviewed minutes from the Application Review Committee and Investment Committee, and interviewed Treasury officials. Our criteria for assessing Treasury's evaluation process drew from GAO's *Standards for Internal Control in the Federal Government* and past GAO work, particularly on CPP.[48]

To describe the characteristics of institutions that applied for and received SBLF program funds, we collected and analyzed data from Treasury. For example, we analyzed the number of institutions that applied; the number of institutions that were approved and nonapproved; the number of institutions that applied to refinance CPP or CDCI funds; and the institutions' geographic locations. To determine the extent to which the distribution of SBLF funds was associated with state unemployment rates, we collected state unemployment rates from the Bureau of Labor Statistics and compared the data against both the number of funded institutions and the dollars of funding by state, using correlations and regression analysis.

We developed a comparable peer group of banks that did not receive SBLF program funds and compared their financial condition and recent small business lending with that of SBLF bank applicants and participants. We analyzed the proportion of loans worth less than $1 million (or less than

$500,000 in the case of farm-related loans) as an indicator a one kind of small business lending. This definition is different from qualified small business lending under SBLF, which includes loans for under $10 million to firms with revenue less than $50 million. Peers were chosen based on size, geographic location, and type of institution. We excluded CDLFs from the analysis comparing applicants and participants with peers. These are not regulated depository institutions, and the lack of supervisory information did not enable us to describe comparable financial characteristics. For certain comparisons of applicants with peers, we omitted problem banks that were ineligible for SBLF so that the two groups would be more comparable. We obtained CAMELS composite ratings from FDIC for both applicants and peers. We assessed the reliability of the data used for our analyses by, for example, reviewing prior GAO work and inspecting data for missing observations and outliers. We found that they were sufficiently reliable to describe the characteristics of SBLF banks and their peers.

To determine banks' **reasons for applying** or choosing not to apply to the SBLF program, we conducted a nationally representative survey of executives of banking institutions with less than $10 billion in total assets.[49] Based on lists of financial institutions provided by FDIC, OTS, and the Federal Reserve, we identified 6,733 institutions with less than $10 billion in total assets to be included in our population for this survey. We selected a stratified random sample of 794 institutions from the population of 6,733 (see table 2). We stratified the population into four strata based on the amount of assets and whether the entity was part of a holding company or a stand alone bank or thrift. The sample size was determined to produce a proportion estimate within each stratum that would achieve a precision of plus or minus 7 percentage points or less, at the 95 percent confidence level. We then inflated the sample size for an expected response rate of 50 percent. Because of the smaller number of banks and holding companies with assets greater than $5 billion and less than $10 billion, we selected all of these with certainty.

We received valid responses from 510 (64 percent) out of the 794 sampled banking institutions. The weighted response rate, which accounts for the differential sampling fractions within strata, is 66 percent. We identified eight banking institutions in our sample that were either closed or were improperly included in the sampling frame. We classified these as out of scope institutions and adjusted our estimates so they are generalized only to the 6,659 (+/- 58) institutions estimated to be in-scope institutions in the population.

Table 2. Population, Sample Size, and Respondent Information for

GAO Survey

Stratum	Population size	Sample size	Out of scope	Respondents within scope
Holding company $5- $10 billion	63	63	2	30
Holding company Less than $5 billion	5,118	378	5	249
Banks $5- $10 billion	5	5	0	4
Banks less than $5 billion	1,547	348	1	219
Total	**6,733**	**794**	**8**	**502**

Source: GAO survey results.

The Web-based survey was administered from June 15, 2011 to August 15, 2011. Bank executives were sent an e-mail invitation to complete the survey on a GAO Web server using a unique username and password. Nonrespondents received several reminder e-mails and a letter from GAO to complete the survey. The practical difficulties of conducting any survey may introduce additional nonsampling errors, such as difficulties interpreting a particular question, which can introduce unwanted variability into the survey results. We took steps to minimize nonsampling errors by pretesting the questionnaire with four banks in April 2011. We conducted pretests to make sure that the questions were clear and unbiased and that the questionnaire did not place an undue burden on respondents. An independent reviewer within GAO also reviewed a draft of the questionnaire prior to its administration. We made appropriate revisions to the content and format of the questionnaire after the pretests and independent review. All data analysis programs were independently verified for accuracy.

To assess Treasury's plans to monitor participants and measure SBLF's effectiveness, we interviewed Treasury officials about their intended work. To describe trends in small business credit markets, we used a number of indicators to describe market conditions before and during the implementation of SBLF. These indicators included data from a survey conducted by the National Federation of Independent Business on whether members' borrowing needs are being satisfied; a survey by Wells Fargo addressing banks' ease or difficulty in obtaining credit; and the Federal Reserve's bank survey on the cost of credit for loans of various sizes. For additional information on current credit market conditions, we also used data from a Federal Reserve's survey of large banks (Senior Loan Officer Opinion Survey) and an estimate of small business loan originations developed by Thomson Reuters and PayNet. To determine the reliability of these data sources, we relied on previous GAO work and interviewed company representatives as appropriate to learn about their data collection methods and any changes to their controls. Based on our analysis we determined that, while the individual sources were not independently crucial to our findings, they were sufficiently reliable together to document patterns in the small business credit markets.

We conducted this performance audit from December 2010 to December 2011 in accordance with generally accepted government auditing standards. Those standards require that we plan and perform the audit to obtain sufficient, appropriate evidence to provide a reasonable basis for our findings and conclusions based on our audit objectives.

Appendix II. Responses to Questions from GAO's Survey on the SBLF Program

We distributed a Web-based survey to 794 banking institutions from the population of 6,733 to determine whether they applied to the SBLF program and the reasons for their decision.[50] We received valid responses from 510 (64 percent) out of the 794 sampled institutions. Tables 3-7 below show the responses to questions from the survey. Because we followed a probability procedure based on random selections, our sample is only one of a large number of samples that we might have drawn. Because each sample could have provided different estimates, we also provide the lower and upper bound estimates at a 95 percent confidence interval. The weighted response rate, which accounts for the differential sampling fractions within strata, is 66 percent. For more information about our methodology for designing and distributing the survey, see appendix I.

Table 3. Has your bank applied, or does it plan to apply, to the SBLF program?

Responses	Estimated percentage	95 percent confidence interval-lower bound	95 percent confidence interval-upper bound
Yes, we applied.	18	14	22
Yes, we plan to apply.	2	<1	3
No	80	77	84

Source: GAO survey results.

Table 4. What are the reasons your bank had for applying for funding through the SBLF program?

Responses		%	95 percent confidence interval-lower bound	95 percent confidence interval-upper bound
It is a source of capital to meet growing demand for small business credit.	A reason	94	86	98
	Not a reason	6	2	14
It is financially attractive in relation to the expected cost of capital relative to market alternatives.	A reason	91	81	97
	Not a reason	9	3	19
It offers the ability to refinance Capital Purchase Program (CPP) funds through the SBLF program.	A reason	31	20	44
	Not a reason	69	57	80
Other			18	68
			32	82

Source: GAO survey results.

Note: Examples of "Other" responses included the program offering a source of capital to grow and Tier 1 capital treatment.

Table 5. Of all the reasons your bank had for applying for funding through the SBLF program, which one was the most important reason for applying?

Responses	%	95 percent confidence interval-lower bound	95 percent confidence interval-upper bound
It is a source of capital to meet growing demand for small business credit.	41	29	52
It is financially attractive in relation to the expected cost of capital relative to market alternatives.	35	23	46
It offers the ability to refinance Capital Purchase Program (CPP) funds through the SBLF program.	18	9	29
Other	7	2	16

Source: GAO survey results.

Note: Examples of "Other" responses included the program offering a source of capital to grow and Tier 1 capital treatment.

Table 6. What are the reasons your bank had for NOT applying for funding through the SBLF program?

Responses		%	95 percent confidence interval-lower bound	95 percent confidence interval-upper bound
We have little or no anticipated demand for small business credit.	A reason	42	36	47
	Not a reason	58	53	64
We plan to avoid taking on new obligtio ns during current economic conditions.	A reason	22	17	26
	Not a reason	78	74	83
We prefer to avoid participation in government programs.	A reason	50	44	55
	Not a reason	50	45	56
The SBLF was less financially attractive in relation to the expected cost of capital relative to market alternatives.	A reason	28	23	34
	Not a reason	72	66	77
The terms of participation were unfavorable.	Not a reason	36	30	41
	Not a reason	64	59	70
The application process was too burdensome.	A reason	32	27	37
	Not a reason	68	63	73
Other	A Reason	38	30	47
	Not a reason	62	53	70

Source: GAO survey results.

Note: Examples of "Other" responses included not being eligible to apply for the program or not needing additional capital at the time.

Table 7. Of all the reasons your bank had for NOT applying for funding through the SBLF program, which one was the most important reason for NOT applying?

Responses	%	95 percent confidence interval-lower bound	95 percent confidence interval-upper bound
We have little or no anticipated demand for small business credit.	29	24	34
We plan to avoid taking on new obligations during current economic conditions.	5	3	7
We prefer to avoid participation in government programs.	25	20	30
The SBLF was less financially attractive in relation to the expected cost of capital relative to market alternatives.	8	5	11
The terms of participation were unfavorable.	9	6	13
The application process was too burdensome.	6	4	9
Other	18	14	22

Source: GAO survey results.

Note: Examples of "Other" responses included not being eligible to apply for the program or not needing additional capital at the time.

End Notes

[1] House Committee on Small Business, *The State of Small Business Access to Capital and Credit: The View from Secretary Geithner*, 112th Cong., 1st sess., 2011.

[2] Pub. L. No. 111-240, 124 Stat. 2504 (2010).

[3] In this report, "banks" refers to banks, thrifts, and bank and thrift holding companies. For the purposes of the SBLF program, a CDLF is an entity that is certified by Treasury as a community development financial institution (CDFI) loan fund. CDFI is a specialized financial institution that works in market niches that are underserved by traditional financial institutions.

[4] S. 681, 112th Cong. (2011). On April 6, 2011, members of the House also introduced a bill to give TARP's Special Inspector General oversight of the SBLF. H.R. 1387, 112th Cong.(2011).

[5] The Dodd-Frank Act eliminated the OTS, which chartered and supervised federally chartered savings institutions and savings and loan holding companies. Rulemaking authority previously vested in the OTS was transferred to the OCC for savings associations and to the Federal Reserve for savings and loan holding companies. Supervisory authority was transferred to the OCC for federal savings associations, to the FDIC for state savings associations, and to the Federal Reserve for savings and loan holding companies and their subsidiaries, other than depository institutions. The transfer of these powers was completed on July 21, 2011, and OTS was officially abolished 90 days later (Oct. 19, 2011). 12 U.S.C. §§ 5411-5413.

[6] The CAMELS rating system is a U.S. supervisory tool that describes a bank's overall condition and that is used to classify the nation's banks. The composite rating is based on financial statements and regulators' on-site examinations and has six components—capital adequacy, asset quality, management, earnings, liquidity, and sensitivity to market risk—that make up the acronym. It rates banks on a scale of 1 to 5, with 1 being the strongest. Evaluations of the six CAMELS components take into consideration a bank's size and sophistication, the nature and complexity its banking activities, and its risk profile.

[7] GAO, *Standards for Internal Control in the Federal Government*, GAO/AIMD-00-21.3.1 (Washington, D.C.: November 1999).

[8] Community Development Capital Initiative (CDCI) is part of the TARP program that makes capital available to certain certified CDFIs for the purposes of increasing lending to small businesses and other community development projects.

[9] The weighted response rate accounts for the differential sampling fractions within strata. More information can be found in appendix II.

[10] A call report is the common reference name for the quarterly reports of condition and income filed with regulators by every national bank, state-chartered Federal Reserve member bank, and insured state nonmember bank.

[11] Treasury's guidance also excludes loan portions guaranteed by the Small Business Administration and those for which a third party assumes risk.

[12] The problem bank list is a confidential list created and maintained by the FDIC listing banks that are in jeopardy of failing. In general, "problem" institutions are those institutions with financial, operational, or managerial weaknesses that threaten their continued financial condition. Depending upon the degree of risk and supervisory concern, they received a composite CAMELs rating of either "4" or "5".

[13] Some banking institutions areformed as either S-corporations (S-corps) or mutual organizations (mutuals) which will affect the form of Treasury's investment. An S-corporation makes a valid election to be taxed under subchapter S of chapter 1 of the Internal Revenue Code and thus does not pay any income taxes. Instead, the corporation's income or losses are divided among and passed through to its shareholders. *A mutual organization* is a company that does not issue capital stock and, therefore, has no shareholders. It is also "owned" by its

members (e.g., deposit customers) rather than by stockholders. Many thrifts and insurance companies are mutuals. Insurance companies are not eligible to participate in SBLF.

[14] The capital is in the form of Tier 1 capital for banks that issue preferred stock to Treasury. Tier 1 capital is considered the most stable and readily available capital for supporting a bank's operations. It covers core capital elements, such as common stockholder's equity and noncumulative perpetual preferred stock. The SBLF funds are Tier 2 capital for institutions that are subchapter S Corps and Mutuals and that issue subordinated securities to Treasury. According to the June 13, 2011, interim final rule from the Federal Reserve, S-Corp and Mutual bank holding companies with less that $500 million in consolidated assets may exclude the SBLF subordinated securities from debt. CDLFs issue unsecured equity equivalent capital that does not constitute a class of stock or represent equity ownership in the issuer.

[15] Treasury may require matching private capital and limit SBLF funding to 3 percent of risk-weighted assets. Risk-weighted assets are weighted according to credit risk and are used in the calculation of required capital levels. Specifically, all assets are assigned a risk weight according to the credit risk of the obligor or the nature of the exposure and the nature of any qualifying collateral or guarantee, where relevant. Off-balance sheet items, such as credit derivatives and loan commitments, are converted into credit equivalent amounts and also assigned risk weights. The risk weight categories are broadly intended to assign higher-risk weights to—and require banks to hold more capital for—higher-risk assets, and vice versa. See 12 C.F.R. Part 3 (OCC); 12 C.F.R Part 208 and Part 225, App. A & B (Federal Reserve); 12 C.F.R. Part 325 (FDIC); and 12 C.F.R. Part 567 (OTS).

[16] As the number of applications increased over time, Treasury requested additional support from the regulators. The Federal Reserve, FDIC, and OTS provided a total of four senior financial analysts as detailees, who acted as Treasury employees, to review applicants.

[17] Specifically, OCC used three conclusions: (1) nonobjection, (2) nonobjection conditioned on private capital raised of a specified amount, or (3) unable to support the request for SBLF funding to provide information for Treasury's evaluation. OTS also provided a "positive" or "negative" assessment on each applicant.

[18] SBLF staff also requested input from state banking regulators, but state regulators were not required to provide it.

[19] In particular, the SBLF Program Office reviewed the Small Business Lending Plans to determine if applicants include key information, such as (1) the communities served and the SBLF's ability to meet their lending needs; (2) loan demand in the communities served, including a quantitative assessment by loan or business type; (3) the applicant's historical small business lending growth and experience; (4) participation in Small Business Administration, U.S. Department of Agriculture, or state small business lending programs; (5) the resources that the applicant dedicated to small business lending activities; (6) the role of small business lending within the applicant's overall corporate strategies and business objectives; (7) current qualified small business lending as a percentage of total loan portfolios; and (8) the applicant's use of general media outlets for outreach; and (9) the applicant's targeting of individuals that represent, work with or are women, minorities, or veterans.

[20] These detailees worked as Treasury employees and were compensated by Treasury during their assignment on the Application Review Committee. They were not serving on behalf of their respective regulators.

[21] Treasury used three key performance ratios for evaluating applicants that measured the following types of assets, as a percentage of capital reserves: classified assets, nonperforming loans, and construction and development loans. For a more detailed discussion on the specific parameters for these key ratios, see appendix I.

[22] In our 2010 report on CPP, we found that because Treasury relied on the regulators to make recommendations for CPP investments, it had limited oversight of regulators' reasons for recommending withdrawals from the program. As a result, CPP participants might not have

received equal treatment. We recommended that Treasury establish a process to monitor applicants for programs similar to CPP to ensure that they were treated equitably. For more information on our recommendation, see GAO, *Troubled Asset Relief Program: Opportunities Exist to Apply Lessons Learned from the Capital Purchase Program to Similarly Designed Programs and to Improve the Repayment Process*, GAO-11-47 (Washington, D.C.: Oct. 4, 2010).

[23] Some applicants had less than 30 days to close because Treasury's decisions to approve them were made after August 30, 2011.

[24] We selected key inputs used by Treasury to guide its decisions and performed an analysis for all 935 applicants to determine which applicants, both approved and nonapproved, fell out of Treasury's stated parameters for the various inputs. We did not review the evaluation documents, such as regulator's supervisory consultation memos, minutes from the Application Review and Investment Committees for all 935 applicants. For a more information on our methodology, see appendix I.

[25] For the remaining two, the lending plan was not responsive because the projected small business lending increase was not greater than or equal to amount requested. Treasury's documents indicated that one was rewarded less than what they asked for, and the other one had an amount that was a bit shy of this threshold, but was ultimately approved.

[26] Treasury officials suggested that loss share agreements and other guarantees—that protect banks against risk of losses from certain nonperforming assets—could explain accepted applicants with elevated ratios of nonperforming loans.

[27] Treasury officials noted that a number of the 535 nonapproved applicants withdrew from the application process prior to Treasury's evaluation.

[28] Treasury indicated that they subsequently found that 16 of the 175 applicants either had dividend restrictions or withdrew before Treasury's consideration.

[29] None of these banks had a CAMELS score of 1.

[30] A Treasury IG official told us that the next IG report will focus on Treasury's evaluation process and will review a sample of decisions more in depth, including the role of the repayment probability estimates in Treasury's funding decisions.

[31] Specifically, OCC used three conclusions: (1) nonobjection, (2) nonobjection conditioned on private capital raised of a specified amount, or (3) unable to support the request for SBLF funding to provide information for Treasury's evaluation. OTS also provided a "positive" or "negative" assessment on each applicant.

[32] According to Treasury, they also tried to obtain dividend restriction information from the state regulators. However, state regulators did not consistently report this information, and certain states subsequently decided not to participate in the supervisory consultation process.

[33] Treasury subsequently posted this information on its website in May 2011.

[34] Fifty-three of these applicants would have been ineligible regardless of whether they had dividend restrictions because they did not meet the eligibility criteria established by the act by either being on FDIC's problem bank list or having more than $10 billion in assets.

[35] GAO/AIMD-00-21.3.1.

[36] The $17.4 billion figure was reported in Treasury's submission to the President's 2012 budget.

[37] The amounts for total assets were obtained from the institutions' call reports and exclude CDLFs, which do not submit call reports and did not report total assets.

[38] Statistically, the correlation between unemployment and the amount of funding (or the number of funded institutions) is indistinguishable from zero. More funding did tend to go to states with greater GDP, but there is no relationship between unemployment and the amount of funding even after controlling for state GDP. There is variation in unemployment rates within states, and our analysis at the state level does not account for this.

[39] We developed a peer group of institutions by matching each applicant with an institution in the same general category of institutions (e.g., thrifts) and in the same state. We did not assess banks' individual financial condition; rather, we looked at averages of certain indicators to

make comparisons between the groups. In order to make the two groups more comparable, we also omitted problem banks from both applicants and peers when comparing these groups, as these institutions are ineligible for SBLF. We excluded CDLFs for the analysis of both applicants and peers. The lack of supervisory information for CDLFs did not enable us to describe comparable financial characteristics. For more information, see appendix I.

[40] For risk-based capital ratios, the adequately capitalized minimum is 8 percent and is equivalent to internationally adopted Basel minimums that apply to both banks and bank holding companies.

[41] This definition of small loans is based on regulatory submissions and is different from the SBLF definition, which defines qualified small business lending as loans below $10 million to firms with revenue less than $50 million annually. Regulatory submissions do not include information according the SBLF definition of qualified small business lending.

[42] The comparison of applicants to peer banks excludes problem banks. When we included problem banks in the applicant and peer groups, both had average CAMELS ratings of about 2.5.

[43] GAO conducted a nationally representative survey of 794 banks, thrifts, and bank and thrift holding companies with total assets of less than $10 billion to gather information on their reasons for choosing to apply or not apply for SBLF. The final sample included 794 banks out of a total population of 6,733. 510 banks, or 64 percent, responded to the survey. The weighted response rate was 66 percent.

[44] The Small Business Lending Index (SBLI) is a measure of new loans to small businesses developed by Thomson Reuters and PayNet Inc.

[45] GAO/AIMD-00-21.3.1.

[46] Once risks have been identified, they should be analyzed for their possible effect. Risk analysis generally includes estimating the risk's significance, assessing the likelihood of its occurrence, and deciding how to manage the risk and what actions should be taken. Because governmental, economic, industry, regulatory, and operating conditions continually change, mechanisms should be provided to identify and deal with any special risks prompted by such changes.

[47] In prior reports, we have reported that internal controls are a major part of efficiently and effectively managing a program, and developing a process for monitoring participating financial institutions will be critical to identifying and addressing any potential problems in these institutions' compliance with program requirements.

[48] GAO/AIMD-00-21.3.1.

[49] Banking institutions includes banks, thrifts, and bank and thrift holding companies.

[50] Banking institutions includes banks, thrifts, and bank and thrift holding companies.

In: The Small Business Lending Fund ISBN 978-1-62257-212-0
Editors: J. A. Bell and C. M. Richardson

Chapter 4

SMALL BUSINESS LENDING FUND: INVESTMENT DECISION PROCESS FOR THE SMALL BUSINESS LENDING FUND*

Department of the Treasury

ABBREVIATIONS

CDCI	Community Development Capital Initiative
CDFI	Community Development Financial Institution
CDLF	Community Development Loan Fund
CPP	Capital Purchase Program
FBA	Federal Banking Agency
FDIC	Federal Deposit Insurance Corporation
FRB	Federal Reserve Board
OIG	Treasury Office of Inspector General
SBA	Small Business Administration
SBLF	Small Business Lending Fund
TARP	Troubled Asset Relief Program

* This is an edited, reformatted and augmented version of the Audit Report, Office of Inspector General, OIG-SBLF-11-001, dated May 13, 2011.

May 13, 2011

Don Graves, Jr.
Deputy Assistant Secretary for Small Business, Housing, and Community Development

This report presents the results of our audit of the investment decision process for the Small Business Lending Fund (SBLF) and provides an overview of the program's status. SBLF is a $30 billion fund that was created to provide capital to community banks with assets of less than $10 billion with incentives to stimulate small business lending. Our audit objectives were to determine whether: (1) the decision process established by Treasury ensures that eligible institutions in need of capital or with the most potential for small business lending are approved, and (2) investments are made in institutions with good track records for performance and compliance with small business lending requirements.

At the time of the audit, Treasury had established an investment decision framework, but major elements of the framework had not been finalized, providing the Department of Treasury Office of Inspector General (OIG) an opportunity to recommend improvements early in the development stage. Therefore, our audit focused largely on the first two stages of the process that were most defined—the initial eligibility check and Federal Banking Agency (FBA)[1] consultation, which were finalized in March 2011. We reviewed pre-decisional policies and procedures for other stages of the investment decision process, but sufficient information was not available to perform a detailed analysis.

To accomplish our objectives, we reviewed the concept of operations for the decision process, procedural guidance, memoranda of understanding (MOUs) between Treasury and the FBAs, consultative decision templates to be used by the FBAs and evaluation checklists established by Treasury. We also reviewed the program application form, outreach guidance to eligible institutions, and program terms. We interviewed SBLF program staff, contractor personnel, and officials from each of the FBAs. The interviews with the FBAs involved discussions about their processes for determining the financial viability of institutions applying for capital under SBLF. In addition, we met with officials from the Small Business Administration (SBA) to discuss potential lender performance and compliance data as well as small business lending market statistics that could be shared with Treasury officials. We conducted our fieldwork from January through March 2011 in accordance with *Government Auditing Standards*. Appendix 1 contains a more detailed description of our objectives, scope, and methodology.

RESULTS IN BRIEF

Treasury launched the SBLF program on December 20, 2010, but has not issued the program terms for all applicants. Currently, only insured depository institutions, bank holding companies, and savings and loan holding companies may apply for funding under the program. As of April 18, 2011, Treasury had received 626 applications from these institutions requesting approximately $9.2 billion. Approximately 43 percent of the applications were from Troubled Asset Relief Program (TARP)[2] banks. Treasury officials estimate program terms will be released for S corporations, mutual institutions, and Community Development Loan Funds (CDLF) in May. Although it is too early to tell how many institutions will ultimately apply to the SBLF program, Treasury expects that less than two-thirds of the $30 billion will be requested.

As of April 8, 2011, Treasury has also not finalized its investment decision process for evaluating SBLF applications. Treasury submitted applications to the FBAs for review as early as January 2011, but it did not finalize the terms of the FBA reviews until March 15, 2011. Although many areas of the process are still incomplete, Treasury expects to fund the first institutions in the second quarter of calendar year 2011.

Our review disclosed that Treasury's investment decision process, which closely follows legislative requirements, targets institutions that are at least adequately-capitalized because the Small Business Jobs Act of 2010[3] restricts participation to financially viable banks. Financially viable banks are adequately capitalized, not expected to become undercapitalized and not expected to be placed into conservatorship or receivership. According to Treasury officials, this requirement will increase the likelihood that participants, including banks currently participating in TARP capital programs, can repay their investment and have sufficient capital with which to increase small business lending. However, TARP banks approved for SBLF funding are not expected to get much additional capital beyond their outstanding TARP investment balances. The maximum investment for TARP banks, like other institutions, is restricted to a percentage of their risk-weighted assets, and for many TARP banks, such assets may have declined due to the downturn in the economy since the time of their application to TARP.

To a lesser degree the process focuses on the applicants' ability to achieve their small business lending goals. Applicants are required to submit small business lending plans that include their small business lending goals, but neither the FBAs nor Treasury intend to review the plans for the likelihood of goal achievement. Treasury program officials also do not have a formal plan to consult with SBA or leverage market data that SBA may collect to determine the attainability of goals reported even though the Small Business Jobs Act provides that Treasury may consult with SBA regarding the administration of the SBLF program. SBA officials stated that they welcome consultation with Treasury as it would provide an opportunity to: (1) help Treasury maximize SBLF program outcomes; and (2) put institutions in touch with SBA resources for developing outreach plans and business strategies to target small businesses in the areas they serve. Finally, Treasury does not plan to consider the small business lending history of applicants who are SBA lenders to identify institutions with compliance issues. Senior Treasury officials indicated they are interested in having the SBLF program office explore ways to leverage SBA's data and experience to achieve program outcomes.

Our audit also identified other areas where the investment decision process could be strengthened. Specifically, we determined that: (1) although FBAs are required to disclose only material supervisory issues, they have significant discretion on which issues to disclose to Treasury; (2) Treasury has provided no specific guidance to the FBAs for identifying banks that may be required to raise matching funds; (3) the noncumulative treatment of SBLF dividends, which are driven by capital requirements imposed by an amendment to the Dodd-Frank Wall Street Reform and Consumer Protection Act of 2010 (Dodd-Frank Act)[4], may result in institutions not fully paying all of the expected dividends for Treasury's investment; and (4) the financial performance of applicants may change between the time of the FBA review and the disbursement of funds, creating a need to update supervisory information provided by the FBAs.

We are recommending that Treasury report to Congress monthly aggregate data regarding the capital ratios of applicants approved for SBLF funding, which is publicly available in call reports. We are also recommending that Treasury evaluate the reasonableness of small business lending plan goals before making investment decisions and consult with SBA in making the evaluation. Treasury should also discuss with SBA compliance issues associated with SBLF applicants who are SBA lenders; confirm with FBAs that there are no changes in an institution's financial viability or new supervisory concerns prior to disbursement of SBLF funds; and develop matching capital guidance for the FBAs detailing Treasury's expectations.

In addition, we are suggesting that Congress consider whether a legislative amendment to the Small Business Jobs Act or a waiver from provisions of the Dodd-Frank Act is needed, to make the repayment of all dividends a requirement for exiting the program.

SMALL BUSINESS LENDING FUND

Program Eligibility

The SBLF is a $30 billion fund created by the Small Business Jobs Act to stimulate small business lending by providing capital to community banks with under $10 billion in assets. Banks with total assets of $1 billion or less may receive capital investments equaling up to 5 percent of their risk-weighted assets. Banks with total assets of more than $1 billion may receive investments of up to 3 percent of their risk-weighted assets. The SBLF also provides an option for eligible banks to refinance preferred stock previously issued to Treasury under two TARP initiatives—the CPP and the CDCI programs. To be eligible for refinancing, an institution must be in material compliance with its CPP or CDCI agreement, be current on its dividend payments to Treasury, and have not previously missed more than one dividend payment. In addition, all outstanding CPP and CDCI securities must be refinanced, with SBLF funds, or repaid in full at the time of the SBLF investment. If approved for less SBLF funding than their outstanding TARP investments, institutions must also pay the difference, ensuring that the TARP investments are repaid in full.

An institution is not eligible for the SBLF program if it is on the FDIC's problem bank list or has been removed from the list in the previous 90 days. Generally, this will include any bank with a composite CAMELS[5] rating of 4 or 5. Treasury may also require some institutions to raise matching funds as a condition for program approval. Banks seeking refinancing of their CPP or CDCI securities cannot be considered for approval on a matching funds basis.

An institution interested in applying for funding must submit an application to Treasury and a small business lending plan to its FBA, which includes the institution's lending goals, the basis for the goals, and how it intends to use the funds to increase small business lending.

SBLF Investment

Treasury will provide participating institutions with capital by purchasing Tier 1 qualifying preferred stock or equivalents in each institution. The price an institution pays for SBLF funding will be reduced as the bank's qualified small business lending increases. The increases in small business lending are measured against a baseline of outstanding loans in the four quarters ending June 30, 2010. As defined by the Small Business Jobs Act, qualified small business lending comprises loans of up to $10 million to businesses with under $50 million in annual revenue within the following categories:

- Commercial and industrial loans;
- Owner-occupied nonfarm, nonresidential real estate loans;
- Loans to finance agricultural production and other loans to farmers; and
- Loans secured by farmland.

The cost of capital provided through SBLF would start at no higher than 5 percent, and could fall to as low as 1 percent depending on the institution's increase in small business lending. For every 2.5 percent increase in the institution's qualified small business lending, the initial 5 percent dividend rate would drop by 1 percent. The dividend rate would be adjusted quarterly for approximately the first 2 years (9 calendar quarters), and then be locked in for the next 2.5 years. Rate reductions would apply only to the portion of the SBLF investment that is equal to the dollar amount of the increase in small business lending. For example, if an institution received an SBLF investment of $5 million and increased its qualified small business lending by $4 million, the reduced dividend rate is applied only to the $4 million.

If an institution does not increase its small business lending in the first 2 years, the cost of SBLF capital rises to 7 percent. If a CPP or CDCI institution refinances under SBLF, but fails to increase small business lending after approximately the first 2 years (10 calendar quarters), the cost of capital will increase by an additional 2 percent annually for the next 2.5 years. After 4.5 years, the dividend rate for all SBLF participants becomes 9 percent.

Program Status

Treasury officially launched the SBLF program on December 20, 2010, approximately 3 months after the Small Business Jobs Act was signed. Although the application process was opened to most institutions in December 2010, Treasury has received only 626 applications, requesting approximately $9.2 billion as of April 18, 2011. Although it is too early to tell how many institutions will ultimately participate in the SBLF program, it is unlikely that all of the $30 billion authorized for the program will be requested if the current rate of applications submitted continues. Treasury currently expects to distribute only one-half to two-thirds of the $30 billion authorized for the program.

Of the total applications received, 271, or 43 percent, were from institutions currently participating in TARP CPP and CDCI programs. The amount requested by TARP applicants is $5.9 billion, or 64 percent of the total funds requested to date. Of the total 626 applications received, 431 were submitted to the FBAs and applicable State regulators for review. The FBAs have completed their reviews of 40 applications. As of May 9, 2011, no applications had completed the other stages of Treasury's review process needed for an investment decision.

At the time of program launch, Treasury released the program terms for only C corporations. The majority of insured depository institutions, bank holding companies, and savings and loan holding companies are C corporations. These institutions were originally given until March 31, 2011, to apply, but this date was recently extended to May 16, 2011. Treasury has not yet established the terms of participation for S corporations, mutual institutions, and CDLFs, as policy changes may be needed regarding either the type of securities that Treasury would purchase from these institutions, or the criteria under which these institutions would be evaluated.

According to Treasury officials, under Internal Revenue Service (IRS) rules, S corporations can have only a single class of stock (common shares). Consequently, these institutions cannot issue preferred stock to Treasury. As a result, Treasury is considering purchasing subordinated debt from these institutions, which the FBAs would likely designate as Tier 2 capital. Treasury officials believe that providing Tier 2 capital would probably result in fewer S corporation participants, as it is unlikely that such institutions would pay the program interest rates for this type of capital.

Additionally, because mutual institutions do not issue stock, Treasury will be unable to receive preferred stock as consideration for an investment in this type of institution. Therefore, Treasury is considering purchasing subordinated debt from these institutions as well.

Treasury must establish alternative means for evaluating the financial viability and repayment ability of CDLFs, which are not regulated or reviewed by the FBAs. Treasury officials stated that they are retaining an outside agent to perform due diligence reviews of CDLF applicants, and developing specific criteria for repayment analyses. In addition to developing the terms for S corporations, mutual institutions, and CDLFs, Treasury –as required under the statute– must also issue regulations to permit the refinancing of CPP and CDCI securities. Treasury has drafted the regulations, and plans to issue them as interim final rules in late spring 2011. Until then, Treasury will be unable to approve applicants attempting to refinance CPP and CDCI investments through SBLF.

At the time of our audit, Treasury had developed, but not finalized all components of the SBLF investment decision process. For example, although Treasury began sending applications to the FBAs in January 2011, it did not reach agreement on the form of consultation to be provided by the FBAs or enter into an MOU with them until March 15, 2011. Representatives from the FBAs told the OIG that they planned to employ the same review process of SBLF applicants as they had for TARP applicants. However, despite expectations of significant similarities between TARP and SBLF processes, it took Treasury several months of negotiations with the FBAs to reach agreement on the type and form of consultation. The parties needed to resolve whether the FBAs would be recommending approval for investment, confirming whether an applicant's CAMELS rating was valid at the time of application, validating the future viability of the applicant, or predicting the probability of loss of the investment. There was also discussion among FBAs regarding the definition of viability and whether viability is a moment-in-time analysis or predictive.

Treasury and the FBAs ultimately agreed that FBAs would advise Treasury only on the financial viability of applicants and their capacity to increase small business lending, and that they would not make investment recommendations as they had for TARP. It was agreed that an applicant would be considered "viable" if it was (1) adequately capitalized; (2) not expected to become undercapitalized; and (3) not expected to be placed into conservatorship or receivership. Further, the FBA's validation of viability of an applicant would reflect only currently available supervisory information and rating assessments at the time the validation was made and would not predict Treasury's loss from making an investment in the institution.

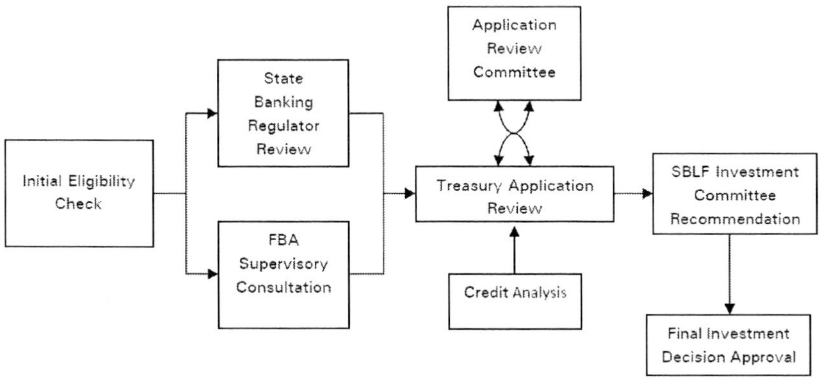

Source: SBLF Action Memorandum diagram (February 2011).

Figure1. SBLF Investment Evaluation and Decision Process.

Additionally, policy documents and evaluation guidance for the other steps of the investment decision process were still in draft form as of late March 2011. For example, Treasury had not finalized review checklists and guidance to be used by the Treasury Application Review Team and Application Review Committee. Further, Treasury began working on a conceptual framework for operations in November 2010, but had not formally documented the controls for the various stages of its investment decision process until late March 2011.

Treasury expects that it could take over 120 days for institutions to receive funding after submitting an application. The investment decision process would take 2 to 3 months, and an additional 30 days or more would be needed for the closing and funding processes, including calculation of the baseline level of small business lending and initial dividend rate.

Investment Decision Process

Since November 2010, Treasury officials have been working to define and implement activities that will support its "concept of operations" for SBLF, which was jointly developed with a third-party contractor. This operating model leverages the investment decision process developed for the TARP CPP and CDCI programs and tailors it for the SBLF program. The most significant difference between the TARP and SBLF process is that FBAs will not manage the application process or recommend institutions for investment. Additional information regarding the difference between the TARP and SBLF programs can be found in Appendix 2.

Under the concept of operations shown in Figure 1, all SBLF applications will undergo an 8-step investment evaluation and decision process, except that CPP and CDCI banks will not be considered for approval based on matching funds.

Initial Eligibility Check

The SBLF Investment Team will perform an initial eligibility check based on publically available information to determine whether the applicant meets program eligibility requirements. Specifically, the team will verify that the institution has: (1) less than $10 billion in assets; (2) requested funding totaling no more than 5 percent of its risk-weighted assets if total assets are less than $1 billion, or no more than 3 percent of its risk-weighted assets if total assets exceed $1 billion; and (3) applied at the appropriate ownership level. If the applicant is refinancing its CPP or CDCI position, Treasury will also confirm that the institution has not missed more than one dividend payment and is in compliance with the terms of its TARP CPP or CDCI capital program.

FBA Supervisory Consultation

As required by the Small Business Jobs Act, Treasury will consult with the appropriate FBA[6] for each eligible institution to determine whether the applicant meets the financial requirements for SBLF eligibility. The designated FBA will determine whether the applicant has a CAMELS composite rating of 3 or better, and has not been on the FDIC problem bank list within the last 90 days. The FBA will also validate the applicant's financial viability based on current confidential supervisory information, which includes examination results, financial ratings, and financial performance ratios. In the event that an applicant is owned by a holding company with multiple subsidiaries, or has significant on- or off-balance sheet activities, the FBA responsible for the bank holding company will also consider the rating and performance ratios at the holding company level and provide a separate consultation to Treasury.

The FBA's validation of viability does not constitute a recommendation that Treasury should invest in the applicant, as Treasury is responsible for ultimately making the investment decision. Instead, the FBAs may inform Treasury on material supervisory issues, including risk management and compliance issues, on-going concerns regarding the financial condition of the institution, the enforcement actions placed on the institution, and any other issues that it believes are not consistent with the receipt of a capital investment. The FBA may also advise Treasury on whether an institution should be required to raise matching capital as a condition of participation in the program. The FBAs may modify their supervisory input at any time before the investment is made. Treasury will not consider an application without a positive validation of viability from the appropriate FBA.

In addition to consultation on the institution's financial viability, FBAs will review the small business lending plan of each applicant from a safety and soundness perspective. The purpose of this review is to assess the applicant's ability to manage the projected increase in small business lending.

State Banking Regulator Review

State banking regulators will also be given the opportunity to review and comment on the financial condition of the applicant; however, their input is not required.

Application Review Committee

The Application Review Committee is a deliberative body made up of current banking supervisors detailed to Treasury. The role of the committee is to ensure that the supervisory consultation process is applied effectively across SBLF investment decisions, and provide recommendations to Treasury on certain SBLF applicants as an additional control point and quality assurance mechanism. The Application Review Committee will review institutions that:

1) Have a composite CAMELS/Rating for Financial Institution (RFI)[7] rating of 3;
2) Have a composite CAMELS/RFI rating of 2 for which the most recent examination is more than 12 months old or for which subsequent quarterly offsite reviews suggest potential deterioration;
3) Have a composite CAMELS/RFI rating of 1 or 2 but have one or more adverse performance ratios;
4) Are required to raise matching capital as a condition of participation as deemed by the appropriate FBA;
5) Do not meet the minimum acceptable probability of repayment in the credit analysis;
6) Receive supervisory input from their State banking regulator that is inconsistent with that of the FBA; or

7) Are otherwise recommended for review by the Treasury Application Review Team (or by the appropriate FBA).

In addition, the Application Review Committee will be asked to review any application that does not receive a positive supervisory consultation. However, the Application Review Committee will not review any application that has been determined to be ineligible to receive capital from the program.

Credit Analysis

Financial agents under contract with Treasury will perform a credit analysis to assess the probability of repayment of the SBLF investment. Institutions must have at least an 80 percent probability of repayment to qualify for the program. A critical part of this analysis will be a forward-looking projection of the institution's cash flows (earnings). In projecting cash flows, the financial agents will review each applicant's asset quality, capital structure, capital adequacy and access to funding, earnings power, and business model. Treasury's financial agents will also consider the institution's forward ratio of Tier 1 common equity to risk-weighted assets, which Treasury believes to be the most statistically significant factor in predicting bank defaults.[8]

In addition, financial agents will perform targeted topical and industry research on the small-cap bank sector to provide Treasury with industry trends and developments relevant to the credit sector. In these cases, the information provided will not be specific to a given applicant and would not be a direct input to the investment decision process for any one applicant.

Treasury Application Review

The Treasury Application Review Team (will prepare a recommendation memorandum for the SBLF Investment Committee based on a review of (1) the supervisory consultation provided by the FBAs, (2) input from the Application Review Committee, (3) the probability of repayment analysis provided by the financial agents, (4) the opinions of State banking regulators, where applicable, (5) the institution's small business lending plan, and (6) other available non-public inputs, if applicable.

SBLF Investment Committee Recommendation

A 5-member Treasury Investment Committee will consider the Application Review Team's recommendation and the institution's application package and will issue a recommendation to the Secretary, or designee. In making its recommendation, it can also request additional information from any previous step of the application process. The committee will be chaired by the SBLF Program Director and staffed by representatives from the Offices of Financial Institutions, Financial Markets, and Economic Policy.

Final Investment Decision Approval

The Secretary, or designee, will review the Investment Committee's recommendation and make the final investment decision.

THE PROGRAM TARGETS INSTITUTIONS WITH ADEQUATE CAPITAL FOR LENDING AND REPAYMENT, BUT SMALL BUSINESS LENDING POTENTIAL WILL NOT BE FULLY ASSESSED

Treasury's investment decision process, which closely follows legislative requirements, targets financially viable institutions. Treasury officials believe that this restriction will ensure that banks approved for SBLF funding have the capital needed to repay Treasury's investment and to increase their loans to small businesses. Although the Small Business Jobs Act requires applicants to submit plans outlining goals for increasing small business lending, neither Treasury officials nor the FBAs will evaluate the likelihood of goal achievement.

Capitally-Impaired Banks Are Ineligible for the Program

According to Treasury officials, the SBLF program is designed to target those banks with sufficient capital to repay Treasury's investment and to increase small business lending. Under the terms established by the Small Business Jobs Act, only banks with composite CAMELS ratings of 1, 2, or 3 are eligible for the SBLF program. Composite ratings of 1 or 2 are given to banks with the strongest performance based on capital adequacy, asset quality, management, earnings, liquidity, and sensitivity to market risk. Financial institutions with a composite CAMELS rating of 3 exhibit some degree of supervisory concern in one or more component areas. Only those banks in the three highest CAMELS rating categories that are then determined by the FBAs to be financially viable will be considered for an investment. A determination of financial viability means that the bank is adequately capitalized, and is not expected to become undercapitalized. If supervisory input is received indicating capital inadequacy or other concerns about banks rated 1, 2, or 3, Treasury may approve such banks contingent on receipt of matching capital prior to funding. Treasury officials expect to rarely invoke the matching capital requirement.

Further, CPP and CDCI institutions will not be allowed to raise matching capital to meet qualification requirements. These institutions will have to qualify based on their current capital structure, which includes their remaining TARP funds, and be designated as financially viable by their FBA. For some of the TARP banks, the SBLF investment will simply replace the amount of funds invested under TARP. Therefore, institutions refinancing are not likely to receive much, if any, additional capital with which to make small business loans. According to a Treasury official, most of the TARP banks that have applied for SBLF to date have requested capital investments that are only 10 to 30 percent more than their remaining TARP balances.

We believe the investment decision process established by Treasury to be consistent with legislative eligibility requirements. However, to provide greater transparency into the types of institutions approved for program funding, Treasury should report to Congress monthly aggregate data regarding the capital ratios of approved applicants. While we recognize that Treasury cannot share supervisory information provided by FBAs on program applicants, we believe it can and should include in its monthly reports publicly available information from call reports on the capital ratios of banks at the time they are approved for SBLF funding. By doing so, the Congressional oversight committees can be kept informed of whether the program is reaching intended recipients.

Potential for Growth in Small Business Lending Will Not be Fully Assessed

As currently designed, the investment decision process does not consider whether applicants will be able to achieve their small business lending goals. As required by legislation, each institution that applies for an SBLF investment must submit a small business lending plan to its respective FBA, or for state-chartered banks, to its State banking regulator. Based on guidance issued by Treasury, the plan must identify the institution's small business lending goals, describe how the applicant's business strategy and operating goals will allow it to address the needs of small businesses in the areas it serves, and outline its outreach plan for attracting borrowers.

Although the small business lending plan is a vital part of an institution's application for the program, neither the FBAs nor Treasury intend to review the likelihood of participants meeting their small business lending goals. The FBAs will review the small business lending plans from only a safety and soundness perspective, assessing whether applicants have the capacity to increase small business lending. However, the FBAs stated that assessing the plan for compliance with SBLF program features should be Treasury's responsibility.

Further, Treasury will review the plans to determine only whether they:

- Include a representation that the applicant will make qualified small business loans in an amount that is equal to or greater than Treasury's SBLF investment.
- Address the needs of small businesses in areas it serves (and describe those needs and the mechanisms it will use to address them).
- Provide the appropriate linguistic and cultural outreach to attract borrowers (and describe one or more mechanisms for such outreach).

Treasury officials do not believe that the reasonableness of an institution's small business lending plan should be a deciding factor for approval as the Small Business Jobs Act does not require participants to increase their small business lending. Further, officials believe that the legislation incents banks to increase small business lending through dividend reductions (or a dividend increase in the event an institution fails to increase lending) to drive the small business lending gains the program sets to achieve.

Because the Small Business Jobs Act provides that Treasury may consult with SBA in administration of the SBLF program, we met with SBA officials to determine how SBA could help Treasury in the investment decision process. We learned that SBA may conduct market research that could help Treasury determine the demand for small business loans in various geographic areas. SBA also has data identifying the volume of the small business lending of various SBA lenders that may be applying to the SBLF program. SBA could help institutions develop outreach plans and business strategies to target and attract small businesses in the areas they serve, as well as provide other types of technical assistance. SBA officials indicated they welcomed consultation with Treasury's SBLF staff as it would provide an opportunity for them to work together to maximize SBLF program outcomes.

Although SBLF participants are not required to increase lending to small businesses, stimulating such lending was clearly the intent of Congress in creating the SBLF program. Therefore, we believe it would be prudent for Treasury to ensure it is investing in banks with the greatest potential for increasing small business lending. Senior Treasury officials indicated that they have been communicating with SBA and are interested in having the SBLF program office explore ways to leverage SBA's data and experience to achieve program outcomes. Further, they acknowledged that their initial focus was on the financial viability and capacity of applicants to responsibly manage growth in small business lending, and are now planning additional steps to ensure that applicants have credible and specific small business lending plans.

SBA Lending History Will Not Be Considered

Treasury officials expect that some lenders applying to the SBLF program may have participated in loan guarantee programs administered by SBA. SBA officials stated that through its oversight and portfolio analysis functions, SBA collects information that could inform Treasury of institutions that are not in compliance with SBA's lending requirements. Such noncompliance would include institutions making loans to businesses that do not qualify as small, are not using loan proceeds as agreed to, and are not making the required equity injection, among other things. Consequently, such information could help alert Treasury to institutions with a history of noncompliance or over-reporting their small business lending.

Despite the availability of such information and indications from Treasury that its Application Review Team may consider other non-public inputs, Treasury has not incorporated steps into the investment decision process to identify current SBA lenders or consulted with SBA to obtain information on the compliance of those lenders with Federal SBA lending requirements.

OTHER OPPORTUNITIES FOR IMPROVEMENTS

Supervisory Consultation Memo Does Not Require thorough Disclosure

The supervisory consultation memo focuses primarily on performance ratios and CAMELS ratings. The memo allows the FBAs to provide discussion of material supervisory issues in the form of supporting comments in an optional narrative. This allows the FBAs to have significant discretion on the type of information to provide to Treasury. This level of information may have been sufficient under the process established for TARP because the FBAs were responsible for recommending institutions for funding, and thus were stakeholders in the TARP decisions. However, under SBLF, FBAs will not be stakeholders and will not be recommending investments. Rather, Treasury will be making the investment decision; and therefore, will need more robust information with which to make a decision. For this reason, we believe that Treasury should explicitly request more robust information about material supervisory issues for each institution, such as the institution's compliance history, enforcement actions taken against it, and matters requiring attention identified by regulators so that Treasury can make a more informed investment decision.

Criteria for Determining Whether Matching Funds Will be Required Has Not Been Defined

Treasury officials have not provided guidance as to the circumstances that will warrant a matching capital requirement, but believe that the requirement will rarely be imposed under SBLF as it was rarely applied under the TARP CDCI program. They stated that undercapitalization is most likely an indicator of other problems impacting the institution's financial viability that would prevent an applicant from being approved. Further, Treasury has not issued prescriptive guidance to the FBAs to use in making such determinations because it believes that matching capital will not necessarily improve the supervisory review of the FBAs, and the Application Review Committee will address whether matching capital requirements have been consistently applied.

We believe that the Application Review Committee review will be an effective way to identify inconsistency in decisions involving matching capital as Treasury will ultimately make the decision. However, without guidance from Treasury, FBAs may not identify all of the institutions that should be considered for the matching requirement.

Although the FBAs and Treasury's Application Review Committee, Application Review Team, and Investment Committee can all impose the matching capital requirement, we believe that defined criteria for the FBAs would add clarity to an important aspect of the legislation and the investment decision process.

The Non-Cumulative Treatment of Dividends May Result in Institutions Not Fully Paying Dividends Owed on Treasury's Investment

Under the terms set by legislation, dividend payments are non-cumulative, meaning that institutions are under no obligation to make dividend payments as scheduled or to pay off previously missed payments before exiting the program. This dividend treatment differs from the TARP programs, in which many dividend payments were cumulative. This change in dividend treatment was driven by changes in capital requirements mandated by the Collins Amendment to the Dodd-Frank Act.[9]

The amendment equalizes the consolidated capital requirements for Tier 1 capital of bank holding companies by requiring that, at a minimum, regulators apply the same capital and risk standards for FDIC-insured banks to bank holding companies. Under TARP, the FRB and FDIC treated capital differently at the holding company and depository institution levels. The FRB treated cumulative securities issued by holding companies as Tier 1 capital, while FDIC treated non-cumulative securities issued by depository institutions as Tier 1 capital. In order to comply with the Dodd-Frank Act requirement that securities purchased from holding companies receive the same capital treatment as those purchased from depository institutions, Treasury made the dividends under SBLF non-cumulative.

Additionally, given that Tier 1 capital must be perpetual and cannot have a mandatory redemption date, the 10-year repayment period[10] in the Small Business Jobs Act cannot be enforced. However, to encourage repayment, Treasury has placed the following additional requirements and restrictions on participants who miss dividend payments:

- The participant's CEO and CFO must provide written notice regarding the rationale of the board of directors (BOD) for not declaring a dividend.
- No repurchases may be affected and no dividends may be declared on any securities for the applicable quarter and the following three quarters.
- After four missed payments (consecutive or not), the issuer's BOD must certify in writing that the issuer used best efforts to declare and pay dividends appropriately.
- After five missed payments (consecutive or not), Treasury may appoint a representative to serve as an observer on the issuer's BOD.
- After six missed payments (consecutive or not), Treasury may elect two directors to the issuer's BOD if the liquidation preference is $25 million or more.

Treasury believes that both the considerable reputational risk of non-payment and the program incentives for payment will help mitigate the use of a non-cumulative security in the SBLF program. We agree that Treasury's equity investment is consistent with the legislation and that it has reasonably structured the program to incentivize payment of dividends.

However, because dividends are non-cumulative under the Small Business Jobs Act, Treasury has no recourse to require dividend payments as a condition for exiting the SBLF program unless Congress were to amend the Small Business Jobs Act to clarify whether all dividends must be repaid upon exiting the program and/or seek a waiver from the Collins Amendment to the Dodd-Frank Act. We note that Section 171(b)(5) of the Dodd-Frank Act fully exempted securities issued to the Federal government before the end of the TARP investment period on October 4, 2010, from the capital treatment provisions added by the Collins Amendment. This exemption allowed Treasury to receive cumulative securities under TARP.

RECOMMENDATIONS

Based on our audit of the SBLF investment decision process, we recommend that Treasury:

1) Report monthly to Congress aggregate data on the capital ratios of institutions at the time they are approved for SBLF funding, which is publicly available in call reports.

   Management Response

   Treasury officials agreed with this recommendation and stated they will include aggregate data on publicly-available regulatory capital ratios in the monthly transaction reports published for SBLF.

   OIG Comments

   Management's proposed actions are responsive to the OIG's recommendation.

2) Consult with SBA in making investment decisions to determine the achievability of small business lending goals and identify compliance associated with applicants who are or were SBA lenders.

   Management Response

   Treasury officials agreed with the OIG that information regarding the performance record of current or former SBA lenders applying for SBLF funding could serve as a useful input to SBLF investment decisions. Following consultation with the OIG, Treasury initiated discussions with SBA in early March to obtain access to this information. While these discussions are ongoing, Treasury officials indicated they would welcome the opportunity to incorporate such data into SBLF investment decisions.

   Treasury officials also stated they are implementing a comprehensive review process for small business lending plans to ensure that SBLF applicants submit responsive plans that establish specific lending goals. In this context, officials stated they will continue to explore ways in which the SBA could support Treasury's assessment of these plans. They reported that to date, the applicability of SBA market research with respect to SBLF has been limited because:

   1. SBLF is a new initiative that is designed to foster increased credit availability by providing banks with the financial capacity and incentives to increase small business lending in local markets. These forward-looking effects may not be fully incorporated in retrospective analyses of market demand.
   2. The conventional bank lending market addressed by SBLF has not been correlated with SBA lending in recent years due, in part, to the economic downturn and temporary enhancements to SBA programs (e.g., increased guarantee levels and fee waivers).

Consequently, measures of an institution's SBA lending may not be indicative of potential lending increases under SBLF.

3. SBA lending programs and associated reports employ materially different definitions of "small business lending" and underwriting standards than those that are statutorily mandated for SBLF. These differences yield the potential for significant inconsistencies in comparisons of SBA and SBLF lending patterns.

Treasury appreciates this recommendation and will continue to assess additional ways in which SBA resources could supplement Treasury's evaluation of applicants' small business lending goals.

OIG Comments

Management's proposed actions are responsive to the OIG's recommendation.

3) Identify opportunities where SBA can provide technical assistance to institutions to help increase small business lending and maximize program outcomes.

Management Response

Treasury officials agreed with this recommendation. They stated that since the passage of the Small Business Jobs Act, Treasury and SBA officials have worked in tandem to coordinate the agencies' implementation of the Act, including briefings regarding SBLF program terms and status for SBA leadership and field office staff.

As institutions begin to receive SBLF funding, Treasury officials anticipate there will be additional opportunities to further deepen these relationships and foster collaboration among SBA, Treasury, and SBLF participants to maximize the program's results.

OIG Comments

Management's proposed actions are responsive to the OIG's recommendation.

4) Modify the supervisory consultation form to require that FBAs provide more robust information on applicants beyond performance ratios and CAMELS ratings, such as history of compliance, enforcement actions, and matters requiring attention.

Management Response

Treasury officials indicated that they share the OIG's interest in ensuring that comprehensive supervisory input is made available for each applicant, and they have consulted the FBAs regarding this recommendation.

They stated that the supervisory consultation memorandum requires the FBAs to complete a written narrative for each applicant with respect to material supervisory issues, including the on-going financial condition of the institution and enforcement actions, if any. According to Treasury officials, the FBAs have indicated to Treasury that the types of information cited in this recommendation constitute material supervisory issues that would be subject to inclusion in the supervisory consultation memorandum. In addition, the FBAs have told Treasury officials that they complete multiple internal reviews of each consultation prior to submission. Treasury officials stated that they also conduct a review of each consultation upon receipt to further validate the information provided.

OIG Comments

Although management officials did not agree to modify the supervisory consultation form to specify the types of information that must be in the narrative, the OIG considers Treasury's comments to be responsive. However, the OIG will follow-up to ensure that the FBAs are reporting all material supervisory issues on the supervisory consultative memorandum.

5) Establish a process that confirms with the FBAs that there has been no change in the safety and soundness or viability of the applicant, and that there have been no new supervisory concerns identified prior to disbursement of funds for all applicants.

Management Response

Treasury officials generally agreed with this recommendation, indicating that they have implemented such a procedure. According to Treasury officials, the FBAs notify Treasury on an ongoing basis as they are made aware of material information regarding an applicant that becomes available following submission of the supervisory consultation memorandum. In addition, Treasury also monitors each applicant's public filings to assess any changes in its financial condition.

OIG Comments

The OIG does not believe that monitoring public filings is an effective way to identify material supervisory issues that may occur subsequent to the supervisory consultation as such issues may not be made public. Also, relying on the FBAs to notify Treasury of changes in material information affecting applicant eligibility may not be the most effective means of obtaining assurance that approved applicants remain eligible. We believe that Treasury should exercise greater due diligence by contacting the FBAs prior to funding to confirm there has been no change in the financial viability of applicants as FBAs may forget to notify Treasury of any changes and will not have knowledge of the timing of Treasury's funding decision.

6) Develop matching capital guidance for the FBAs that detail Treasury's expectations of the FBAs with both general principles and specific parameters. Include sample scenarios that can demonstrate the types of factors that should warrant consideration of matching funds – e.g., ranges of performance ratios, individual CAMELS component ratings, etc.

Management Response

Treasury officials indicated that they maintain an ongoing dialogue with the FBAs regarding the supervisory consultation process for SBLF, including the application of the matching capital provision.

Based on these discussions, Treasury officials indicated their understanding is that there are only limited circumstances – often unique to a specific institution – in which the addition of matching capital alone would alter an FBA's viability assessment. This is because weakness in an institution's regulatory capital position is most frequently a consequence, and not a cause, of deficient performance with respect to other supervisory elements such as management, asset quality, and earnings.

Examples of situations Treasury has reviewed with the FBAs for which matching capital may be appropriate include certain institutions that have experienced: (1) significant losses in their securities portfolio, the source of which would not otherwise prompt concerns regarding investment or asset-liability management practices, (2) a temporary impairment arising from a natural disaster or similar finite event, and (3) historical losses that have reduced capital levels, even as the institution has resolved legacy asset quality challenges and returned to profitability.

In line with this recommendation, Treasury officials agreed to document these scenarios in written guidance. Because many such situations are institution-specific in nature, Treasury officials stated they have also established the policy that the Application Review Committee – a team of experienced banking supervisors detailed to Treasury – will review any application for which an FBA suggests matching capital or does not provide a positive validation of viability.

e purpose of these reviews is to ensure that the supervisory consultation process is effectively applied across all applications, including those for which matching capital may be relevant

OIG Comments

Management's proposed actions are responsive to the OIG's recommendation.

MATTER FOR CONGRESSIONAL CONSIDERATION

We are suggesting that Congress consider whether an amendment to the Small Business Jobs Act and/or waiver from the Collins Amendment to the Dodd-Frank Act is needed to make the repayment of dividends a requirement for exiting the program.

We appreciate the courtesies and cooperation provided to our staff during the audit. If you wish to discuss the report, you may contact me at (202) 927-0384.

Debra Ritt
Special Deputy Inspector General for
Office of Small Business Lending Fund Program Oversight

APPENDIX 1. OBJECTIVES, SCOPE, AND METHODOLOGY

We conducted this audit of the Small Business Lending Fund (SBLF) in response to our mandate under section 4107 of the Small Business Jobs Act of 2010.[11] This section provides that the Office of SBLF Program Oversight is responsible for audit and investigations related to the SBLF program and must report at least twice a year to the Secretary of the Treasury and Congress on the results of oversight activities, including recommended program improvements.

We initiated an audit of the investment decision process for SBLF on January 20, 2011, pursuant to Section 4107 of the Small Business Jobs Act. Our objectives were to determine whether the review process established by Treasury ensures that (1) eligible institutions in need of capital or with the most potential for small business lending are approved, and (2) investments are made in institutions with good track records of performance and compliance with Federal lending requirements.

At the time of the audit, Treasury had established an investment decision framework, but major elements of the framework had not been finalized. Therefore, our audit focused largely on the first two stages of the process that were most defined—the initial eligibility check and Federal Banking Agency (FBA)[12] consultation, which were finalized in March 2011. We reviewed pre-decisional policies and procedures for other stages of the investment decision process, but sufficient information was not available to perform a detailed analysis.

To accomplish our objectives, we reviewed the draft concept of operations for the decision process, procedural guidance, memoranda of understanding (MOUs) between Treasury and the FBAs, consultative decision templates to be used by the FBAs and evaluation checklists established by Treasury. We also reviewed the program application form, outreach guidance to eligible institutions, and program terms. Further, at our request, SBLF responded in writing to OIG questions, providing explanations of initial program focus and critical path activities.

We interviewed SBLF program staff, contractor personnel, and officials from each of the FBAs. The interviews with the FBAs involved discussions about their processes for determining the financial viability of institutions applying for capital under SBLF. In addition, we met with officials from the Small Business Administration (SBA) to discuss potential lender performance and compliance data as well as small business lending market statistics that could be shared with Treasury officials.

We conducted our fieldwork from January through March 2011 and prepared this report in accordance with Government Auditing Standards. Those standards require that we plan and perform the audit to obtain sufficient, appropriate evidence to provide a reasonable basis for our findings and conclusions based on our audit objectives. We believe that the evidence obtained provides a reasonable basis for our findings and conclusions based on our audit objectives.

APPENDIX 2. COMPARISON OF TARP – CPP/CDCI AND SBLF

	TARP - CPP/CDCI	**SBLF**
Overall Goal	To stabilize and strengthen the U.S. financial system by increasing the capital base of viable institutions, enabling them to lend to consumers and businesses	To address the ongoing effects of the financial crisis on small businesses by providing temporary authority to the Secretary of the Treasury to make capital investments in eligible institutions in order to increase the availability of credit for small businesses
Authorization	**$700 billion**	**$30 billion**
Structure	An institution's participation in the Troubled Asset Relief Program (TARP) could fall under multiple areas: 1) Capital Purchase Program (CPP) 2) Term Asset-Backed Securities Loan Facility (TALF) 3) Commercial Paper Funding Facility (CPFF) 4) Debt Guarantee and Temporary Liquidity Guarantee Program (TLGP) 5) Troubled Asset Insurance Finance Fund (TAIFF) 6) Community Development Credit Initiative (CDCI)	An institution's participation in the Small Business Lending Fund (SBLF) would only link the entity to SBLF
Participation	No exclusions based on assets No exclusions based on CAMELS ratings No exclusions based on the Problem Bank List Maximum investment under CPP – 3 percent of risk-weighted assets (RWA)[13] capped at $25 billion	Issuer must have total consolidated assets equal to or less than $10 billion as of the end of calendar year 2009 Congress allows CPP/CDCI institutions to refinance into the SBLF Issuer must redeem all outstanding CPP or CDCI preferred stock on or prior to the Treasury investment date All CAMELS 4 and 5 rated banks are excluded Banks that are or have been on the FDIC Problem Bank List within the last 90 days are excluded Maximum investment for issuers with $1 billion or less in total assets or that are Community Development Loan Funds (CDLF)— 5 percent of RWA

	TARP - CPP/CDCI	SBLF
	Maximum investment for issuers under CDCI – 5 percent of RWA	Maximum investment for issuers with $1 billion to $10 billion in total assets or that are required to seek matching private capital investment – 3 percent of RWA
Dividends	Dividends are cumulative or non-cumulative 5 percent annually until the fifth year (CPP) 2 percent annually until the eighth year (CDCI) Following initial 5-year period, rate will be 9 percent (CPP) Following initial 8-year period, rate will be 9 percent (CDCI)	Dividends are non-cumulative Initial rate of 5 percent annually, adjusted quarterly for approximately the first 2 years (9 calendar quarters) based on small business lending. When lending increases: 1) by less than 2.5 percent, the adjusted rate will be 5 percent 2) by at least 2.5 percent but less than 5 percent, the adjusted rate will be 4 percent 3) by at least 5 percent but less than 7.5 percent, the adjusted rate will be 3 percent 4) by at least 7.5 percent but less than 10 percent, the adjusted rate will be 2 percent 5) by 10 percent or greater, the adjusted rate will be 1 percent Following initial 2-year (10 calendar quarters) period, if small business lending has remained the same or decreased, the adjusted rate will be 7 percent Following initial 4.5-year period, the adjusted rate will be 9 percent CDLF -- rate will be 2 percent annually for the first 8 years, then 9 percent
Repayment	No restrictions until 5 missed payments[14]	**For any missed payment**, restrictions will apply including: 1) the issuer's CEO and CFO must provide written notice regarding the rationale of the board of directors (BOD) for not declaring dividends

(Continued)

	TARP - CPP/CDCI	SBLF
	After 5 missed payments (consecutive or not), Treasury may appoint representatives to serve as an observers of the issuer's BOD **After 6 missed payments** (consecutive or not), Treasury may elect 2 directors to the issuer's BOD To repay all or part of the investment, issuer must pay a minimum of 25 percent of the issue price of the preferred stock	2) prohibiting dividends for the applicable quarter and the following 3 quarters **After 4 missed payments** (consecutive or not), the issuer's BOD must certify in writing that the issuer used best efforts to declare and pay dividends appropriately **After 5 missed payments** (consecutive or not), Treasury may appoint a representative to serve as an observer of the issuer's BOD **After 6 missed payments** (consecutive or not), if the liquidation preference is $25 million or more, Treasury may elect 2 directors to the issuer's BOD For CPP participants[15], if at the beginning of the tenth full quarter after investment date, small business lending has not increased, issuer must pay a lending incentive fee of 2 percent annually of the aggregate liquidation preference Lending incentive fee will end 4.5years after the investment date To repay any part of the investment, issuer must pay a minimum of 25 percent of the number of originally issued shares or 100 percent of the then-outstanding shares, if less than 25 percent of the originally issued shares
Restrictions & Requirements[16]	General usage requirement on the capital invested including the expansion of the flow of capital	Capital investment must be used to increase small business lending or suffer increased dividend rate May not invest in a CPP participant that has missed more than 1 dividend payment under CPP Require the issuer to provide linguistically and culturally appropriate outreach and advertising Applicable Federal Banking Agency (FBA) (or the like)

	TARP - CPP/CDCI	SBLF
	Consider factors which include: 1) providing financial assistance to financial institutions, including those serving low- and moderate-income or underserved areas, 2) providing stability and preventing disruption of financial markets, 3) the need to keep families in their homes, and 4) minimizing cost to taxpayers Prior to January 2009, there were no requirements for recipients to report on their use of TARP funds	must issue guidance on underwriting standards to be used for loans made using SBLF funds within 60 days Treasury may take actions the Secretary deems necessary to carry out authority given under the legislation Consider factors which include: 1) providing funding to minority-owned eligible institutions and other institutions that serve minority-, veteran-, and women-owned as well as low- and moderate-income, underserved, or rural areas, 2) increasing the opportunity for small business development in areas with high unemployment, 3) providing funding to eligible institutions that serve communities that have suffered negative economic effects due to the 2010 offshore drilling unit failure along the coast of the Gulf of Mexico, and 4) minimizing cost to taxpayers Treasury must provide a written report to Congress detailing how participants have used the funds received under the SBLF, within 7 days after the end of each quarter Quarterly reporting requirement for recipients and recalculation of dividend
Application Review Process	No required state input Advisory board members (CPP Council) are FBA representatives	Requires consultation with appropriate FBA (or the Community Development Financial Institution (CDFI) Fund for non-depository CDFIs) and consideration of state input (if provided) Application Review Committee members are Treasury representatives

(Continued)

	TARP - CPP/CDCI	SBLF
	Applications start with FBAs FBAs provide Treasury with recommendation for investment All analysis performed by FBAs FBA or CPP Council recommendation goes to Investment Committee	Applications start with Treasury FBAs do not provide Treasury with recommendation for investment Credit analysis performed under Treasury Application Review Team receives supervisory input and credit analysis before sending to the Investment Committee Issuer is required to submit a small business lending plan to the FBA or applicable state regulator
Miscellaneous	Programs under TARP did not require a new organization Restrictions on executive compensation No formal outreach performed -- bailout program highly publicized Allows for Treasury to purchase warrants	Requires new program formation and establishment of new organization SBLF is established as separate and distinct from TARP -- Recipient of SBLF capital investment is not as a result also considered to be a recipient of TARP Assurance that if a subsequent change in law modifies the terms of the investment under the Program in a manner that materially adversely affects the issuer, the issuer, after consultation with the applicable FBA, may repay the investment without impediment No restrictions on executive compensation Outreach to banks necessary -- Call center and outreach materials needed No allowance for Treasury to purchase warrants

End Notes

[1] The FBAs are the Office of the Comptroller of the Currency, the Office of Thrift Supervision, the Federal Deposit Insurance Corporation (FDIC), and the Federal Reserve Board (FRB).

[2] The TARP program consisted of several initiatives, which included the Capital Purchase Program (CPP) and the Community Development Capital Initiative (CDCI).

[3] The Small Business Jobs Act of 2010, Public Law 111-240, was signed into law on September 27, 2010.

[4] The Dodd-Frank Wall Street Reform and Consumer Protection Act of 2010, Public Law 111-203, was signed into law on July 21, 2010.

[5] The CAMELS rating system is an international bank rating system through which bank supervisory authorities rate institutions from 1 (best) to 5 (worst) on six components: capital adequacy, asset quality, management, earnings, liquidity, and sensitivity to market risk. Each component rating is weighted and an overall composite rating of 1 to 5 is assigned to each bank. A composite CAMELS rating of 1 is the highest rating and represents the least supervisory concern, indicating the strongest performance and risk management practices relative to the institution's size, complexity, and risk profile. A composite CAMELS rating of 5 is the lowest rating and represents the greatest supervisory concern, indicating the most critically deficient level of performance and inadequate risk management practices relative to the institution's size, complexity, and risk profile.

[6] In the case of CDLFs, which are not regulated, the SBLF program office would consult with Treasury's Community Development Financial Institutions Fund.

[7] According to the Federal Reserve's *Bank Holding Company Supervision Manual*, RFI ratings are the equivalent of a bank's CAMELS ratings, but are applied at the holding company level.

[8] FRB used this ratio in its 2009 stress test of the 19 largest bank holding companies.

[9] Section 171 of Public Law 111-203.

[10] The repayment deadline can be extended or waived if it would adversely affect the capital treatment of the stock or financial instrument.

[11] The Small Business Jobs Act of 2010, Public Law 111-240, was signed into law on September 27, 2010.

[12] The FBAs are the Office of the Comptroller of the Currency, the Office of Thrift Supervision, the Federal Deposit Insurance Corporation (FDIC), and the Federal Reserve Board (FRB).

[13] The risk-weighted asset amount is determined as of the call report immediately preceding the date of application, less the amount of any CDCI investment and any CPP investment.

[14] A dividend payment is considered "missed" after 60 days.

[15] CPP participant refers to an issuer that participated in CPP and did not redeem, or apply to redeem, the CPP investment on or before December 16, 2010.

[16] All reporting requirements of the Program, the Inspector General of the Department of the Treasury and the Government Accountability Office are not listed in this table.

INDEX

D

E

F

G

H

I

Q

R

S